My Neck of the Woods

LOUISE DICKINSON RICH

My Neck of the Woods

DOWNEAST MAGAZINE

CAMDEN, MAINE

DOWN EAST

CAMDEN, MAINE 04843

Contents

My Neck of the Woods

1

The North Country

SPEAKING RELATIVELY, I live in the far north—in the top, left-hand corner of Maine, just below the Canadian border—and there seems to be something about that country that fascinates people, even people who have never been there and never intend to go. Perhaps it's an inheritance passed down through the centuries from the time when for those who ventured away from the known coasts, the familiar landmarks, there was only one fixed point to steer by, the Pole Star, only one sure thing to guide them, the trembling needle pointing North. Or perhaps the North represents an idea, a state of mind, cold, detached, lonely and austere, sanctuary from the heat and confusion and indulgence of the modern world. Or perhaps again—and this is by far the most probable explanation—I'm making much ado about nothing, and the thing that interests chance acquaintances and sets them to asking questions about the North when they find out where I live is nothing more nor less than pure astonishment that anyone could be so misguided, and a natural curiosity about such a life. So I try to tell them what the North is like.

In the first place, it is very, very beautiful. It's a country of lakes and forested mountains and tumbling rivers. It's beautiful all the time. In the spring the new leaves of the birches and the blossoms of the maples look like wisps of green and red smoke blowing across the staid dark background of the fir and spruce, and the forest floor is carpeted with flowers—huge purple violets and tiny white ones, and the fragile wood sorrel, and the pink twin-sisters. The leafless rhodora blazes in the swamps. Then the thrushes sing high on the ridges in the arrowy light from the setting sun, and the red deer come down the slopes, stepping daintily, into the dusk of the valleys to drink. In the little villages and cross-roads around the lofty plateau of the lakes, the ancient lilacs break in a frenzy of bloom like lavender surf over the low houses against which they lean. Even when it rains—and it rains quite a lot in Maine in the spring—it's beautiful. The curtains of the clouds hide the mountains, and all the world is gray and dim and full of the sound of water, and of the high, sweet voices of the peepers in the bogs.

Summer is lovely, too, rich and full-blown. Cool, crisp nights follow blue sun-drenched days. Thunderstorms rattle around the mountains, rolling up one valley and down the next. The wild blueberries and raspberries ripen in hot clearings back in the woods, and the bear and foxes eat their fill. Everything smells wonderful—the pine, aromatic under the sun, the breeze blowing across a rock-ribbed pasture of cut hay, the very earth itself.

You have to see autumn in the North to believe it. The lakes are incredibly blue and the hillsides shout with color—orange and scarlet, yellow, and a crimson that is almost purple. In the night, the wild geese honk overhead beneath a full, burnished moon, fleeing south over the silvered ridges

from the smell of winter. The Borealis crackles up from the
northern horizon, sending unearthly streamers of light a
thousand miles long to waver and fade at the zenith. At sunrise the ground is white with hoar-frost, against which the
tracks of the rabbits and deer and bob-cats are black and pre-
cise, and the water in the ruts of the woodsroad is skimmed
lightly with ice. The air is like wine, thin and dry and chilled;
and like wine, it exhilarates body and mind, so that the performance of great tasks and the dreaming of great dreams
are as easy as turning over your hand.

And winter—what can I say about winter, when the wind,
clean and knife-edged, pours down from the northwest, and
the country is held in the grip of an iron cold? The snow
falls and falls, steadily and soundlessly; or it drives down the
bitter wind, scourging the land. The houses in the villages
huddle together like sheep under its lash. The ice on the lakes
silently thickens—one foot, eighteen inches, three feet—until
it is as solid as living ledge under the heaviest load. In the
dead silence of a windless night, it surrenders to the strain
of its own increasing pressure, and as the rift runs across a
lake—two, four, ten miles—a great half-human howl echoes
through the mountains and up to the stars. It's a blood-chilling
sound to hear, wild and lost and despairing.

It doesn't snow all the time. Between storms the sky is deep
sapphire, and all the shadows on the glittering white earth are
violet. Nothing is familiar. The drifted snow lends grace and
softness even to the stark architecture of a woodshed. In the
villages and cross-roads, the windows of the besieged houses
peer over eight-foot walls of snow at cars passing on the
cleared roads, and every chimney wears constantly a plume of
blue wood-smoke. Men shoveling paths and mittened women

hanging out their stiffly frozen sheets call back and forth, and their voices are clear and bell-like in the crystal air. But winter is more than a time of ice and snow and cold. It's a time when more than the land is drained of life and emotion. It's a time for sitting and thinking, for being quiet, as the trees and rivers and lakes are quiet.

That's what the North is like, I try to tell people, although of course there's a lot more to it than that. Almost nobody could be satisfied to live forever without human contacts, immersed in and sustained solely by natural beauty. That wouldn't be living at all. Such an existence would end in either stagnation, or in madness brought on by the terrible loneliness. There are some, like Elmer Rhodes, who do go mad, although not necessarily from loneliness. But people go insane in cities, too, and who hasn't been lonely at some time during his life, no matter where he lives? Elmer Rhodes was an exception. Cliff Wiggin, my next-door neighbor on the west, five miles down and across the river, sometimes goes for months on end without seeing a soul, and he's far from crazy. He's far from stagnant, too. He's full of ambition and busy as a beaver all the time. But maybe he's an exception, too, and anyhow, nobody wants to hear about Cliff. Everybody wants to know—and they smile insinuatingly and knowingly when they ask—if it isn't true that we backwoodsmen eat fresh venison every month in the year.

It so happens that I never ate a piece of illegal deer meat in my life, partly because I consider it just slightly more palatable than old goat meat, partly because I really disapprove of poaching, and also partly, I must admit, because I'm afraid of the game warden, Leon Wilson. He's a nice guy as long as he's sure you're on his team, but he can get awfully tough awfully fast when he suspects that you aren't. I don't want him getting tough with me, the way he did with Morgan Twitchell— But I've lost my audience, which is demanding how cold it gets in winter.

It gets pretty cold, sometimes, down to forty or more below zero. But most of the time it doesn't get much colder than ten below in the day-time, which is a good snappy temperature in which to work outdoors. Once, though, Alys Parsons and Frances Greenwood and I, with our assorted husbands and hired help, walked the four miles across the lake in twenty below weather, and we were too hot when we got to South Arm, where the road to the Outside begins. Of course there was no wind, and in this altitude the air is dry and doesn't seem so cold, and we were walking pretty fast. Frances had on her new Easter hat, all covered with flowers— but no one is interested in Frances' hat.

No one is interested in Rienza Trimback's aprons, either, or in the Crew twins, or in what happened to Fred Kilgore. They're just people, and people are a dime a dozen Out-in-the-States—which is what we sometimes call the large part of the Union outside the backwater in which we live. People are no treat. Everybody knows hundreds of them, and they're all the same, aren't they? So skip the people, and tell us about the North. Nobody lives there anyhow. That's what makes it so fascinating.

Well, it's always interesting to hear another point of view outlined, as my sister says when she thoroughly disagrees with someone, but doesn't feel up to a fight. I suppose from one viewpoint, five and a half persons per square mile, which is about what we average, does add up to nobody. As for me, I consider that an ideal population, thick enough to be comforting, yet not so thick as to be cramping. Some of the five and a half have lived here all their lives, some were born here, moved elsewhere for a while, and then came back, and some came from Away originally to settle here; but they all have a quality in common. I'm not sure whether it's a cause or an effect. To put it in the simple and unflattering words of a friend, Mabel Sias, "Do you people get the way you are from living here, or were you all peculiar to start with? Why you all even look alike."

We really don't, of course, but I can see what she means. There is a prevalence of the long Yankee face, with its lean jaw, uncompromising mouth, and observant eyes, but the universal resemblance is more than that. It lies in the expression on the faces, which do not give themselves over easily to the polite smile or the grimace of facile grief. It lies in the handling of the body—in the deceptively leisurely stride and the economy of gesture, in the almost animal-like ability to relax and to spring from relaxation into action. It lies, too, in the speech, which is laconic, and the manner of speaking, which is deliberate and usually unimpassioned, and I'm afraid, frequently unintelligible to the Outsider. But these are only the visible clues to some fundamental common denominator.

What that denominator is, I find it hard to say; and anyhow, I'm tired of talking about my friends and acquaintances in terms of population averages and generic types, because they're a large part of the reason why I like the North. The landscape is very beautiful, as I have said, but it's the figures in the landscape that make it interesting. To me they are different from people anywhere else I have been, and they make more sense in the things they do and say. Whether this is because there are so few of us here that we know practically everything there is to be known about each other, and so understand almost everything, or whether Mabel Sias is right and it takes an eccentric to understand an eccentric, I'm neither prepared nor willing to state. All I'm going to do is just for once forget about the scenery and the weather and tell about the people.

2

The People Next Door

ONE OF THE very few things that a probably misspent life
has taught me is that no matter how tough the going may
become at times, you do manage to get along somehow,
by the Grace of God and a long-handled spoon. Even so,
I don't see how I could possibly get along without my
next-door neighbors, Alys and Larry Parsons. The very
thought of having to try makes my blood run cold. It isn't
only because of the material aid and comfort they give me,
either. I suppose that if all came to all (the local variation
of "if worse came to worst") I'd be able to get someone
to carry my mail and groceries and freight up and down
the lake, give me a hand at loading a barrel of kerosene into
and out of the back of the Ford, tell me what ails my washing
machine motor when it won't start, and advise me what to
use to get raspberry stains out of a white shirt. But the
people who can do all those things aren't always, or even
very often, people that feel the same way you do about the
country you call home, with whom ~you can arrive at
conclusions through a peculiar, truncated language which
consists as much of what is not said as of what is said, who
agree with you about what is funny and what is sad, or who

can and will play along with you in your simple-minded little games and diversions. The Parsonses are the exceptions. I'd probably be able to maintain life in this feeble frame without them, but I'd be awfully lonesome and I wouldn't have much fun.

The label "next-door neighbor" here doesn't mean the same thing that it does in civilized communities. Al and I don't do any gossiping over back fences as we hang out our washings. We both have pretty good lungs, but not good enough to make shouting over a distance of two uninhabited miles of wilderness feasible. The Parsonses live at Middle Dam proper, where from May through September they operate a sporting camp, and I live down below Lower Dam at Forest Lodge on the Rapid River. We're connected by the Carry Road, which is more of a carry than a road, consisting as it does of rocks and ruts and dilapidated corduroy culverts, and wandering irresponsibly through Black Valley and over Birch Hill and past the Devil's Hopyard to provide a passage between two large lakes—Lower Richardson and Umbagog—the Rapid River being unnavigable for canoes. We're also connected by a catch-as-catch-can telephone line, privately owned by a lumber company, powered by dry batteries, and running about fifteen miles from Middle Dam down along the road, through a swamp and over a mountain to the Brown Farm in Magalloway Plantation. The Carry Road offers no access to the Outside; for that you have to take a boat from Middle Dam across Lower Richardson to the South Arm, where another road takes off for Civilization.

In summer when the hotel, so-called, is open and the mail comes In every day except Sunday, I see the Parsonses at least six times a week, but I don't know them very well. After the first of October, when we go on to our winter schedule of mail on Tuesdays and Fridays only, I see them twice a week, but I know them much better. In winter I talk with Al over the telephone, too, at least once a day. Since Ralph died and the children are Outside at school, I live alone in winter. I have raved and sworn so loudly and at such length on the subject of the criminal folly of anyone's living alone in the woods and making himself a burden and a responsibility to the neighbors that the least I can do, I feel, is to save my own neighbors worry by checking in every twenty-four hours with the information that I'm still alive and kicking. In summer I never call Al up unless I have something important to say to her. She's too busy running her business to welcome idle chat from me or anyone else.

The hotel at Middle Dam is constructed on the general plan of many sporting camps throughout the country. There is a large central building, painted white, wide-porched, and rambling over the greater part of half an acre, which houses the lobby or office, the dining room, the kitchen, and back-hall, or helps' dining room, and on the second floor the sleeping quarters of the women employees. The male employees sleep in the guides' house, up back, and up back, too, are the barns, shop, engine house for the lighting and pump systems, the storehouse, icehouse, woodsheds, and laundry. North and south along the lake shore, spread out like wings from the main building, are the nineteen individual cabins for the guests, each with its own bath and living room, with fireplace or Franklin stove, and from one to three bedrooms. It is really quite a large and elaborate establishment, completely independent when it comes to the common public utilities like light and water, and it requires a great deal of work and thought and ingenuity to keep it running smoothly.

The thought and planning go on all the time, but the concentration of hard labor, as far as the Parsonses personally are concerned, comes in the spring when the place has to be opened for business after a long winter. Then there is only a skeleton staff on the premises, the rotten condition of the ice precludes getting more help In, and there is so much to be done. In Larry's department the boats must be repaired and painted and launched, the plumbing must be overhauled and connected, chimneys and leaky roofs must be patched, and a million minor repairs must be made. He usually has, in addition to his year-round man, Swene Meisener, two or three extra men to help him, and the Lord knows he needs them. Under Al's aegis come the more domestic aspects of opening the place: the cleaning of the cabins, the setting up of the dining room, in which the tables and chairs have all been piled on top of each other to make room for the winter storage of rowboats, the organizing of the kitchen and store-room, and the policing of the flower beds. She usually has one woman to help her, and that woman's time is pretty well taken up in preparing meals for Larry's crew.

So, very often on a nice spring day I go up to help Al, more for her company's sake than anything else. The sight of a dandelion in bloom on a sunny south bank or of snow fleas hopping merrily about on a melting drift, or the wild and disturbing cry of the loons flying up-river in the night to find the first stretches of open water in Pond-in-the-River have sufficiently infected me with spring fever so that I don't want to stay home where I belong. Besides, there is no really good reason why I should stay home. I can do my own house-cleaning any time before the middle of June, when the children come In from school, and the silver lining of the dark cloud of living alone is that you aren't tied down to three meals a day and a ten o'clock bedtime. If you want to leave your breakfast dishes in the sink, shut the drafts of the stove tight, close the door behind you, and walk two miles to help a neighbor wash windows, you are at liberty to do so, returning when you feel like it, be it late that night or not until the next day or the day after.

It was while Al and I were feverishly cleaning Petticoat Alley, the wing of the hotel in which the waitresses and cabin girls sleep, making up beds and hanging fresh curtains, that she said to me a little distraughtly, "I'd certainly like to know how it happened that I woke up one morning and found myself in the hotel business way Back of Beyond. I'm very sure I never planned—" She pounded her thumb with a tack hammer and broke off to shake it and swear.

I laughed, pounded my own thumb, and said, "Damnation!" When order had been restored, I told her, "I know just how it happened. The same way I happened to wake up and find myself a writer living way Back of That. We married the men."

And that, of course, is exactly what did happen. Al, like me, is a native only by circumstance, choice, and—at long last—tenure of office. She was born and lived all her life Out-in-the-States, and probably had every intention of continuing to do so, until her college roommate suggested one summer that they both get jobs way off at this quaint and unlikely place in the woods, just for the fun of it and for something different to do to kill the vacation. So they did, the roommate as a waitress and Al as a cabin girl. I remember seeing her that first summer—my career as a native is a few years longer than hers—walking around with an armload of clean towels or sun bathing on the float. Her name was Alys Grua then, which I thought was one of the strangest and prettiest names I'd ever seen written or heard spoken, and which would probably have been the only thing I knew or remembered about her, if it hadn't been for Larry. At that time Captain and Mrs. Coburn owned and ran the hotel, and Larry had been their boatman in summer and caretaker in winter for several years. He started paying attention to Al, and she was interested enough so that she came back to work the next summer, and the winter after that they were married. She came In to live this odd and sometimes difficult life for the same reason that I did: because the men we married wouldn't be happy anywhere else, and we preferred to be miserable with them than comfortable without them. Or at least that's what we both probably thought at the time. It was so long ago and so much has happened since that it's hard for us to say just exactly how we did feel as brides.

The Parsonses built a very nice little house for their year-round home up above the tennis court, where the Carry Road begins, on the C Township side of the Magalloway line, and they have lived there ever since. I like their house. It stands among the trees, with a lawn and flower bed in front, and flower boxes outside the kitchen. You can look out of their front windows over the roofs of the cabins along the shore and see the whole length and breadth of the lake from the Narrows almost into South Arm, and the great northwest flank of Old Blue, with cloud shadows chasing over it and snow on its summit in the fall when it's raining down below.

It's a view that is never twice the same, but always lovely, no matter what the weather or the season of the year.

For a few years Larry continued to work for Captain Coburn and Al stayed home and ran a gift shop in her living room for the benefit of the guests in summer, and in winter kept house for her husband, like anyone else. Then one fine April day, when the air was soft from the south, shrinking the snow and turning the ice blacker and blacker, word was received from Mrs. Coburn that the Captain had died suddenly on his way home from Florida. There were already reservations for people who were panting expectantly on the Outside, waiting to come In for the spring fishing as soon as the ice was out, and the hotel had to open. The Coburns were childless, so the mantle of proprietorship fell on Al and Larry, and they have continued to wear it to this day, when Mrs. Coburn too is dead.

That's how Al happened to wake up one day and find herself in the hotel business, and I thank God whenever it occurs to me to do so that it's she and not I. But that's all right. I have more than a suspicion that she considers my means of livelihood with the same feeling of inadequacy and horror with which I regard hers. What we have in common is a way of life and a frame of reference in which to conduct our respective enterprises, and a healthy and, I hope, mutual respect for each other's special temperaments and abilities.

I long ago gave up describing my friends to people, because I'm apparently no judge of what they look like. All of my friends are either beautiful or handsome, depending on their sex. They really are, although I'm told that it's just because I'm glad to see them that they look so wonderful. I'm sure Al is a beautiful woman, though, even discounting my natural bias. She is tall and slim and carries herself well, and she wears her clothes with style. I don't pretend to be stylish, so my admiration when she appears looking like something out of *Vogue* is untinged by envy. It does burn me up slightly, however, when she infringes on my sartorial territory of dungarees and plaid shirts, and continues to look chic. I forgive her, though, for the sake of her voice, which is low and flexible, a rare thing among women in this country; and for the sake of her eyes, which are among the loveliest I have ever seen, large and gray-blue and eloquent, with dark lashes; and for the sake of her smile, which contains an almost angelic sweetness, in contrast with her sometimes salty conversation.

She has a way of saying, when I'm stewing and fussing about something, "You certainly have a terrible time, don't you, Louise? And enjoy every minute of it," in an amiable but astringent tone that makes me suspect that I'm raising an awful hoo-rah about nothing. She's very good for me. But over and above all that, she possesses the two qualities which I think I admire and envy above all others, whenever I encounter them. One is great physical courage, which it has become fashionable among those who lack it to rate second to moral courage. I don't. Moral courage is fine, and Al has plenty of that, too; but physical courage is not the common commodity that the books would have us believe, and I am always impressed and moved by any demonstration of it. The other quality is the simple, old-fashioned, and increasingly rare virtue of not being afraid of hard, dirty work. I simply *love* a good worker.

Of course, I think Larry is handsome, in a charming, masculine way. He is dark, and he laughs a lot, giving the impression of great good nature. As is not always the case, this impression is founded in fact, as far as Larry is concerned. He is about the best-natured and most obliging person I have ever known. He's much too accommodating for his own good. People—me included—impose on him terribly. Or at least, they impose on him up to a point. When this point is reached, long after anyone else would have flown into a thousand exasperated bits, Larry is all through for good. After that there's no sense in asking him for favors, because he won't do them, and I admire him for it. I've known him longer than I have anyone else in this country except John Lavorgna, and the longer I know him, the better I like him and the more I respect him. When I was new to this country and didn't realize that according to rural morality it is improper for a woman to entertain affection for any male other than members of her very immediate family, I once made the grave error of stating publicly that I was very fond of Larry. Fortunately the only two people whose opinion mattered to me, Al and Ralph, had been around and understood what I meant; and it didn't seem worth while to explain to the others that our very tenderest passages consisted of Larry's showing me how to fix the faulty generator of my Reo with a bit of zinc out of a common flashlight battery, or of my lending him my three-and-a-half ton chain hoist to haul out the rear end of his Chris-craft.

Larry and I see eye to eye about this country. I remember once in November he was driving me over to Upton to see my children, in school there. We started over East B Hill just as it began to spit a little snow. The leaden clouds, heavy and dull, pressed down almost onto the tops of the trees, and the woods on either side of the narrow dirt road were drab and as still as painted pictures, in the hush preluding the storm, the evergreens black and rigid with frost, the hardwoods bare-branched and lifeless. A little dirty snow lay in ragged patches along the way, and the dank chill of the air penetrated even into the station wagon. It was a bleak and desolate scene, and I shivered involuntarily as I looked out at it.

"It sure looks Godforsaken," Larry remarked. "I don't know why we don't give it back to the Indians."

"I don't either," I agreed. "They didn't know any better, and we do. Or at least we ought to. I never saw such a dreary hunk of geography in my life. And right this minute some people we know are swimming in Florida."

Larry shifted gears as we started to climb toward where the road disappeared into the low-hanging, snow-swollen clouds. "Want to join them?"

"Good God, no!" I exclaimed, appalled at the thought.

"Me neither. This country's not so much to look at, maybe, but it suits me."

Several years later he and Al did go to Florida for a month's vacation. When they returned, looking very brown and healthy, I asked whether they'd had a good time; and it seemed that they had, a very good time indeed.

"But how was it really?" I insisted, entertaining ideas of their having been seduced into desertion by the hot sands of the South while I'd been up to my ears in snow, and practically freezing to death.

Larry shrugged. "Nothing there but climate, and we've got plenty of that at home. Better here, too. More variety to it." And that settled Florida's hash.

To run a business that is in operation only a little more

than four months of the year sounds like a sinecure. It sounds like the lazy man's dream. Sure, you do a little work during those four months, if keeping a few books and giving a few orders to the help and chatting with the guests occasionally can be called work. And think of the other eight months! Nothing to do except loaf and spend the easy profits. It sounds too good to be true; and I have news for anyone who's thinking of trying it: it is too good to be true. I don't know all about it, naturally, but I have been deeply enough involved from time to time with various phases of the business to know that it's no bed of roses.

The first thing to be done in the spring is to get the Ice Out announcements ready to mail. The announcements that the Parsonses send are little folders with the literature describing the camp on the inside, and "The Ice Is Out at Lakewood Camps" on part of the outside. The rest of the outside is reserved for the address. For a week or two after we hear the first crow cawing off somewhere in the woods—the first infallible sign, if not exactly of spring, at least of the prospect of spring some time—Al keeps her typewriter alerted with a stack of announcements and the address book beside it, so that in spare moments while she is waiting for the potatoes to boil or for Larry and Swene to come in from the woodshed, she can address a few more announcements. There are hundreds of the things and it's a terrible chore. In the meantime, on one of his trips for the mail, Larry has bought six or eight sheets of cent-and-a-half stamps, and the plot is that anyone who has time on his hands can sit down and fold the addressed announcements, sealing them shut by folding and pasting a stamp over the free edges. I do that quite a lot while I'm killing time at the Parsonses', because it takes no special intelligence, and you can carry on a conversation at the same time. Al and I have decided a lot of weighty problems while getting the Ice Out announcements ready to mail, such as what to do about the pink sweater with black sequins on it that someone gave her, and whether or not I should let my hair grow. We also decided, after wading through several addresses like 375 W. 57th St., New York 21, N. Y., that we couldn't stand living in a place that was identified merely by a series of numbers and abbreviations. We'd feel as lacking in individuality as cards in a steel index. Give us addresses like Wounded Knee, or Pretty Prairie, Kansas. Or even, for that matter, Middle Dam, Maine.

When the announcements are all sealed and stamped, they are put into an empty canned-milk case and shoved under Al's bed to be forgotten until the ice actually does go out and Larry mails them. I would like to add that it is a good idea to carry a roll of Lifesavers in your pocket at this stage of the game, because the Government glue on cent-and-a-half stamps tastes horrible.

The iris bed *always* needs weeding, but in the spring it is even worse than usual, so while it is still too early to start to open cabins, but warm and sunny enough to make working outdoors a joy, Al and I give it a good cleaning out. It lies in a strategic position, commanding a view of almost every building on the place, as well as the lake and dock. No one can go anywhere or do anything without our seeing him from the iris bed, so we combine the pleasures of accomplishing something and satisfying our curiosity. We can chat with Larry as he goes by with a Stillson wrench to where he is connecting the water pipes to the cabins, shout up to Whit Roberts, mending the hotel roof, to ask if he can see any open water over by the Sandbanks from his vantage point, and annoy Swene, painting boats on the lawn. The weeding of the iris bed is more of a social function than a chore.

It was while we were thus employed one April afternoon that we instituted our Fifty Year Bird Plan. Up to that time we could both identify robins, crows, sea gulls, blue jays, and shelldrakes. I was kneeling on a sportsman's discarded magazine, and discovered that the cover-picture, although it said American merganser under it, was actually nothing but a stupid-looking old shelldrake.

"Ooh, look, Al," I said. "Now when people ask us what kind of ducks those are, we can show off."

"We really ought to know the names of the commoner birds here," she said. "After all, we're natives and supposed to know our own country. People are always asking—"

"My system," I told her truthfully, "is to say it's a yellow-bellied sapsucker if it's small. If it's large, I say it's an osprey. Nobody ever knows the difference."

"Yes, but still— I've bought a bird book," she confessed.

Just then Nugget, the cat, came strolling by with a dead bird in his mouth, so apropos that we considered him an instrument of Fate. We hi-jacked the bird, found the bird book, and identified it as a myrtle warbler. Then we decided that although obviously all small birds were going to be myrtle warblers that summer, we'd learn a new bird a year for the next fifty years, and die ornithologists. The next year I found a dead pine grosbeak, and last year a bird became trapped in the office and we caught it and discovered that it was a redpoll. I don't know what chance is going to provide us with This Year's Bird, but something will doubtless turn up.

After the iris bed, it's time to open a few cabins, enough

to take care of the really eager beavers who come In the minute the lake is free, before the regular cabin girls are ready to take over. I won't go into detail about that; it's just plain house-cleaning, washing windows, brushing down walls, and scrubbing floors. It's at this time that I begin to regard Al with awe. All the blankets and linen and draperies have been washed the fall before and stored in a couple of rooms in the hotel proper, and I go up to where she is sorting them into piles and say, "I've finished Metalluc and I'm ready for the curtains and bedding now."

She sits back on her heels. "Metalluc. Yes. Those blue curtains there belong in Metalluc and the gray foot-blankets. And let's see—the cushions there are slip-covered. Right over on that chair." Since there are nineteen cabins and the draperies are not interchangeable, as the windows differ in size and number, it is important to get the right ones. Al never makes a mistake. The inside of her head must look like the files of the FBI.

Once in a while I think that I've caught her in error, and I say smugly, "These slip-covers that you gave me don't belong in Turnstile. All the chairs there are plain wooden rockers." Then I prepare to gloat in a lady-like manner.

"Are you sure? Oh! That bride and groom we had in Allston in September! He didn't think anything was good enough for her, so he swiped furniture out of unoccupied cabins from all over, when we weren't looking. You'll find the Turnstile chair in there, and when you come to Comfort, there'll be a reading lamp missing. That's in Allston, too. I *wish* people would leave things alone." So I trudge meekly back to Allston, and sure enough, I find it crammed with stuff that obviously doesn't belong there. *I* wish I knew how Al does it.

By the time the ice actually does go out, the place is ready to roll, and I figuratively kiss Al good-bye for the duration. While I'll be seeing her every day throughout the summer, things won't be the same. Our encounters will be brief and business-like transactions dealing with my mail and milk and groceries, or else they'll carry about them the flavor of assignations. It's a very rare occasion when I can catch her alone and free to talk. She's a very busy woman.

Her day starts with a six-thirty breakfast with the help, out in the back-hall, and at six-forty she is tidying the office, vacuuming the rugs, running the dust mop around, straightening magazines, and fixing the flowers. The main dining room opens at seven, and when the guests start streaming in, she's at the desk, putting up the mail, getting her daily shopping list ready, answering questions, and finding a box and a piece of string for the lady who wants to send home to her sister in Philadelphia some attractive moss that she's found. Then she has a little conference with the stage driver (who has left his stage across the lake at South Arm), telling him to stop in at Stevens' after he's left the mail, on his way to Rumford, to see if they have any green corn to sell, to be sure and call at Buster's for the tire Mrs. Rich sent out to be vulcanized, to try to match this sample of blue thread for one of the guests, and above all things not to forget that he's to collect some people who are arriving on the three-thirty train. Then if he has time after he's finished his regular shopping list and stopped at Hood's for the special milk for the Gaston baby, will he go around to the Rumford Public Library and see if he can find a quotation for Judge Endicott.

The Judge thinks it comes from Demosthenes and starts out "Like the diet prescribed by doctors." Anyhow, he says it has something to do with the unsoundness of public relief. The stage driver looks defeated but says he'll try.

By this time it is almost eight-thirty, the time the boat has to leave in order to make mail connections, and the Smiths, who are leaving this morning, are still in the dining room. Al goes in and asks tactfully if their baggage is strapped, so that the cabin boy can take it down to the boat. This has the desired effect of hurrying them up, and she walks out onto the dock with them and sees them off, expressing appropriate sentiments and waving good-bye until the boat is halfway to the Ledge. It's all right then to stop and go back to the office for the list of people who want to lunch out to-day. The back-hall girl, who waits on the helps' table and does the helps' dishes, also puts up the lunches, so Al goes into a huddle with her, imparting the information that while most of the lunches will be standard, there are a few deviations. Dr. Spaulding is allergic to butter. Mr. Peters is a Catholic and to-day is Friday, so give him either egg or tuna salad instead of the ham, and Mrs. Keane wants milk instead of coffee in her thermos. Then she hunts for the chef, who is discovered in the big refrigerator counting lamb chops, and starts taking down the things he's going to need from the storehouse during the day. It's a long list, so she impresses his helper to carry the heavy things, and goes back to consult with Rosella, the pastry cook, about desserts. They decide that everyone likes apple pie, and now about that pudding that didn't go so well last night. It's really good, only of course everybody ordered the strawberry short-cake, so how about running it again under a different name?

That settled, Rosella says, "There's still some coffee in the pot. Here, have a cup along with one of these chocolate doughnuts. I just made them and they came out extra good." So Al pours herself some coffee and bites into a doughnut, just as a cabin boy, shielding his eyes with cupped hands, peers in through the screen.

"Mrs. Parsons in there? Someone wants her on the telephone."

Al runs, leaving her coffee but taking her doughnut with her. It's Joe Mooney at the Brown Farm, saying that the Union Water Power Company wants someone to tow their scow to Upper Dam, and then go over to Mill Brook and pick up a load of lumber. The boatman is at South Arm with the big boat, so that means that Larry will have to go with the half-cabin. No one has seen Larry for at least half an hour, so Al starts looking for him and finds him up in the engine room tinkering on the light plant, which showed symptoms of low blood-pressure or something the evening before. She goes back and arranges to have a lunch put up for him, because there's no telling when he will be back, and decides that maybe now is the time to sneak off home and make her bed and perhaps wash out a few stockings. But the laundress catches her before she can escape, to complain that there's no hot water. By the time they discover it was just a question of not having let it run long enough, one of the cabin girls comes in with the report that the kids in Trail's End have broken a window, and what is she supposed to do about it? Al finds Swene and a piece of glass and some putty, and now it's after eleven and time to type the luncheon menus. Then a canoe trip from a boys' camp lands, demanding post cards, soft drinks and candy bars. She rediscovers the great truth that it takes a twelve-year-old about the same length of time to decide between a Sky-bar and an Oh Henry as it does his father to weigh the merits of a Pontiac against a Studebaker, and before they're on their way again, the lunch hour is half over. Larry won't be back for hours, so she goes into the dining room and eats alone.

Now might be the time to make her own bed, she thinks, and starts maneuvering into a position behind the fireplace chimney from which she can make an unobtrusive exit via the cold drink room and the back door. But the kids from Trail's End troup out of the dining room, announcing that they are going to play ping-pong, and may they have the balls? While she is getting them out from under the counter, the telephone rings. Andover announces that a party of two by the name of Baffinland or something like that is on the way In. No, they're not expected; that's why they stopped to have the call put through; but they want the boat to meet them right away. So Al finds the boatman (long since back from South Arm) who is improving each shining hour by cultivating the vegetable garden, sends him on his way, and goes to tell the north-side cabin girl that she'll be having occupants in Birch Lodge, so will she please check it. As she goes quietly past the iris bed, looking neither to the right nor left in the ostrich-hope that if she doesn't see anybody, nobody will see her, the woman in Sunshine hails her, waving a half-knit sock.

"You said you'd help me when I came to turning the heel."

So Al forgets about making her bed for the time being and about washing stockings for the day. While she is explaining patiently, "No, you slip one, knit two together, knit one, and turn," the Coreys come up a little apologetically.

"We know we should have told you before, but we've decided to picnic out to-night instead of going into the dining room. So just this once could you make an exception and have a lunch put up for us?"

Al refrains from commenting that the Coreys are the fifth exception this week and says she guesses it can be arranged. Then she goes out into the kitchen and puts up the lunch herself, since the back-hall girl, thinking that her work is all done until suppertime, has gone blueberrying with the waitresses. Just as she ties the string around the box, she glances out the window and sees the boat out by the Ledge. That means that the Baffinlands-or-whatever-their-name-is are aboard, and she hasn't done a thing about her face and hair since before breakfast. She dashes out of the kitchen and along the path to her own house as fast as she can—and she can run faster than anyone I ever saw—slams into the house, washes her face, puts on fresh lip-stick, runs a comb through her hair, and races down in time to greet the Baffinlands adequately, although a little breathlessly. She shows them to their cabin, answers their seventy-nine questions, and returns to the office, because it's time to type the dinner menus. The chef comes in to say that he's terribly sorry, but he forgot this morning that he was going to need a new bottle of Worcestershire sauce, and will she please get him one from the storeroom. After that, the Baffinlands come in to register and buy fishing licenses, and in the course of that transaction she discovers that their name is really Boardman; so she goes about for five minutes muttering it under her breath, because she believes it's good business to call people by their correct names. Then the people who went over to B Pond yesterday call up from Lower Dam to say that they are back that far, and will she send the command car down after them. She finds Swene, dispatches him down the Carry, and looks down the lake to see the big boat returning from the Arm. Presumably the guests who were to arrive by the afternoon train are aboard, so she goes down to meet the boat, greet them, and get them settled. The B Pond people drive into the yard, jubilant over the fish they have caught. She admires them extravagantly, although she's seen seven thousand fish in her hotel career, and never did think they were particularly fascinating phenomena in the first place. But she shows the fishermen where the fish-box is, and explains that they can send word to the chef by their waitress as to when and how they want the fish cooked.

Just as she has got around to sorting the mail, I come in from down the road, and she says, "Hi. Your tire is out by the iris bed, and here's your mail. What have you been doing all day?"

"Oh, I've been working like a dog," I tell her complacently. "I've finished a chapter of my book, and done some washing, and made bread. Then I finally got my tomato plants tied up, and picked a couple of quarts of raspberries, and of course went swimming with the kids two or three times. I've done a lot. And what have you accomplished for your country?"

"Nothing," she tells me bitterly. "I've just frittered the whole day away. I haven't even made my bed."

That's what goes on with Al all summer long, when things are running smoothly; but sometimes a little sand gets into the gear-box. The laundress has a bilious spell, for instance, and Al has to do the laundry. Or the white-dishwasher goes to her cousin's funeral, and Al does the dishes. Things like that.

The Parsonses used to have an elderly gentleman named Dean working for them, tending the garden, milking the cows, and driving the old car that carries fishermen to the more remote pools along the river. I liked Dean a lot. He was a little teched, as we say, and given to charming illusions. He told me once in the fall that he'd seen sixteen snow-white foxes running a foot race along the shore of the lake in the early morning—purtiest sight he ever see against the deep blue of the water and the scarlet of the maples. Of course it was all in his head, but I thought how lucky he was to have a head like that. One Christmas he made some enormous wreaths and long swags of trailing pine and black alder berries and hung them all over the barn, because he thought that the horses and cattle, whose kind had been present at the birth of the Christ child, should share in the season's celebration. I thought that was a lovely idea; but possibly I wouldn't have been so enchanted with Dean if he'd been working for me, since one of his illusions was that there was no need of his writing anything down, because he had a good memory. Actually he had a memory like a sieve.

He would come into my house and say, "Louise, you seen anything of a couple of sports?"

"Sure, I've seen eight or ten go by to-day. What do yours look like?"

"They got on red-and-black checked shirts." Since nine out of ten sports wear red-and-black checked shirts, this wasn't very helpful. "I'm supposed to pick them up and take them back to the hotel."

"When and where?" I'd ask.

"Seems to me 'twas four o'clock at Lower Dam. Yes, that's what 'twas. Maybe I better write it down." And he'd get out his note-book and stub of a pencil and lean on my ice-box and write down, "Lower Dam, four P.M.," and go away. In about an hour Al would call me up to ask if I'd seen anything of Dean.

"Sure, he was in here a while ago. He said he had to pick up some people at Lower Dam at four o'clock."

"Oh, Lord! They wanted to be picked up at the Hopyard at two. They're going to be furious and I don't blame them."

"I'll run up to the dam and tell him," I'd offer, and she'd thank me.

When I'd delivered the message, Dean would look disgusted. "Pity folks can't make up their minds and keep them made up," he'd snort. "Look, I got it written down right here, Lower Dam, four P.M. Sports are all hen-heads is what I think." During his regime, Dean certainly gave variety and interest to Al's day.

As to what Larry does all summer, I have only a vague idea. Every time I ask where he is, he's either driven to Portland to pick up the Lyonses off the night train, or he's taking a party to Pine Island, or he's helping the electrician fix the mangle in the laundry, or he's asleep because he was up all night taking the man who had a heart attack to the hospital. The few times I do lay eyes on him toward the end of the summer, all he'll talk about anyhow is the World Series and what I think of the Red Sox' chances. He goes temporarily insane every fall, along with most of the guests, male and female. Al and I share a complete indifference to the ability of one group of overgrown schoolboys to hit a ball harder and oftener than another group can, and after having listened to that sort of nonsense far too long and patiently, we have developed a defense. When someone starts, "I've just been listening to the ball game. It's the last of the eighth, Yankees at bat, two on and one down," we move in with our counter-offensive.

"I've just been listening to the radio, Louise," Al will say. "Pepper Young's Family at bat, with Portia Facing Life on third."

"The boy to watch is Young Doctor Kildare," I'll tell her, "although John's Other Wife is batting over three hundred. Do you suppose The Goldbergs will really trade The Woman in White?" While this doesn't precisely endear us to the fans, it does sometimes discourage them a little from talking about baseball, to us at least, and is one of the silly games we play to make life tolerable.

Finally the hotel closes for the season and everything that was taken out for use in the spring has to be washed and ironed and put back into storage. The pipes have to be dis-connected and drained, and everything freezable has to be taken out of the storehouse and put into guides' house cellar. The windows of all the cabins have to be checked and unlocked, because the buildings heave with frost in the winter and unless the window sashes are free to move a little, all the glass will be cracked by spring. It's just as much work to close a camp as to open it, but there is a different attitude toward the whole thing. We have fun in the fall. We all feel free and irresponsible. The summer is over, none of the guests has drowned, the pressure is off. I can go up to see Al any time I want to, knowing that even if she is washing blankets, I won't be bothering her. I can help her, and then we can bum a cup of coffee from the cook and take it outdoors to drink in the sun. Everyone is in fine careless fettle in the fall.

The only time I ever saw Al really mad, though, was in

the fall. I went up the Carry one afternoon and found her sitting on her steps with her hands clasped over her knees, staring out over the lake with a grim expression on her face. "What ails you?" I asked diffidently.

After a minute she said tightly, "You know those damn horses."

I knew the damn horses well, and I knew that she didn't feel much more kindly toward them than I did. They're really nice animals, but they're what is known in this country as gawmy. That means well-intentioned, but clumsy and accident-prone. What I had against them was that the week before Larry had told me that if I wanted some carrots, I was free to take what I cared to dig in his garden. So I found a spading fork and went to work. I big-heartedly decided to dig them all, take the few I wanted, and sack up the rest for the Parsonses. My plan was to go down the rows digging, leaving them lying on the ground, and then to go back and pick them up. When I reached the end of the first row, which was about fifty feet long, and turned around to go back up the next, I found Prince breathing down the back of my neck with the top of the last carrot I'd dug dangling attractively from the corner of his mouth, and Chub right behind him. I'd forgotten that Larry lets them out of pasture in the fall. They'd followed me right down the line, eating carrots as fast as I uncovered them. I was mad, so I banged them over the noses with the fork handle and they galloped away, laughing at me. But the minute I started digging again, they came back and I couldn't get rid of them, so I had to give up.

What Al had against them was this: For some strange reason, she can't learn to braid her hair. She is about the most capable person I know, not only when real labor or brainwork is involved, but in handicraft as well. So it strikes me as being amusing and rather appealing that braiding, which even I can do, baffles her. She decided one day to try doing her hair coronet style, and being unable to braid herself, she appealed to Larry. He said he didn't know how to braid either. But a few days later she surprised him up in the barn braiding the horses' manes and tails, simply to make them look pretty. Larry is really a little soft about those horses; but she thought, and so do I, that if he could braid them, he could braid her. So the horses were slightly in disgrace already on the day that Al lost her temper.

She had spent the whole morning laundering the white sash curtains from the cabin bedrooms, about forty pair, and instead of hanging them on the lines, she'd spread them on the grass to bleach. The next thing she knew, someone had let the horses out and they had not only walked all over the curtains, muddying and tearing them, but had finished the job by lying down and rolling all over them. They were a mess. When I found her, she was trying to make up her mind whether to shoot the horses or shoot herself. In the end, of course, she did neither; but now no one lets the horses out of the pasture without first asking Al if she's planning to bleach curtains.

Now we're in the eight months of the year when hypothetically the owner of a summer resort can relax and cultivate his ethos. There is a great difference between hypothesis and practice in this country, however. It takes until November to get snugged down for winter, with the houses banked, the gardens cleaned, the boats stored, and all tools and equipment under cover. Then there are still eighty-five cords of wood

—more, if it's been a cold summer that has depleted the supply
—to cut, haul, saw, split, and stack, and tons of ice to be put
up. Those jobs, along with incidental chores and emergencies
that are bound to crop up, fill the winter very nicely. Larry
sacrifices two days of every week to the carrying of the mail.
In summer this is simply a matter of going to Andover by
boat and car, and in deep winter, although it isn't quite that
easy, it still can be done safely enough, provided that you're
sufficiently rugged to stand the trip across the lake in a twenty-
below gale. Larry is. He can and frequently does take the kind
of physical pounding that would kill a moose.

But nobody is immune from the dangers of the thin ice of
the fall, and so twice a week until the ice is safe, he has to
walk the mail around the shore. This just about doubles the
four-mile trek to the Arm, and it's a horrible trip. The rocks
are covered with glare ice, and the going is rough. You look
at a point two hundred feet and two minutes away, test the
ice, know it won't hold, and struggle three-quarters of a mile
around a deep cove. I've walked around the shore to get Out,
and my tongue was dragging by the time I reached the Arm. I
wasn't carrying a seventy-pound pack-sack, either, and I didn't
have to turn around and come back the same way the same
day.

Larry's courage, stamina, and sweet temper were demonstrated yet once again on the day that Wade Thurston was
killed. It was late in the day and already dark when he got In
with the mail, and he looked tired, as well he might. He had
just taken off his boots and put on dry socks and slippers
when the telephone rang. It was Joe Mooney to tell Al that
Wade had been killed by a runaway sled. "And will some of
you folks get word to Lee Thurston? He's logging up on

Elephant Back, and they want him to come right Out. I hate to ask you this time of night, but he hasn't got a phone yet, and you're nearest."

Larry was stretched out reading the paper, with the look of a man all settled in for the evening about him, when Al gave him the message. "Jesus, that's too bad," he said. "Poor Wade." He reached for his boots and started putting them on again. "I can't wait for supper. Could you make me a sandwich and some coffee, Al?"

"Oh, Larry," she protested, "you can't go. You've already walked the shore twice to-day, besides the trip to Andover. Can't you send Swene or Louis? It must be an eight-mile walk onto Elephant Back, after you get off the lake. It's too much—"

Larry stood up, tucked in his shirt, and tightened his belt. "Nope, I can't ask the boys to do a chore like this. I don't pay them that kind of money, and I'm not expecting it of them. On top of the trip, which is going to be long and hard enough, it's not going to be any easy chore to break the news to Lee. This is one of those things a joker has to do himself." He drank a cup of coffee. "Where's my good flashlight? It's going to be blacker'n the inside of God's pocket up on that mountain. Well— Expect me when you see me, and don't worry. I might have to go Out to Andover with Lee. He's going to take this hard."

We watched the little spark of the flashlight move slowly along the dark shore of the lake, growing smaller and smaller against the black and starless immensity of the night, disappearing now and then around a point of land, and then reappearing and always going steadily forward. Finally, when we could see it no longer, I said to Al, "Want to know something? You're married to one hell of a swell guy."

She kept her eyes fixed on the point in the darkness where we'd last seen the light. "Do you think that's any news to me?" she asked. She did her ironing that night, knowing that it would be senseless to go to bed to lie tossing and worrying about Larry. Of course, he got back all right the next day; but that's the sort of thing that makes living in the woods hard, much more than the inconvenience and physical effort involved.

Sometimes I used to wonder, before I knew her well, what the percentage for Al was in this life. She was used to civilization, where the flick of a finger floods a room with light and a call to the laundry takes care of the problem of clean sheets. Here we spend hours a week trimming and filling lamps, and washing their chimneys, and at least a day and a half a week getting the dirty clothes washed and out and in again and ironed and put away. In winter it's more than that, because you can't dry them outdoors half the time, so you spend the rest of the week playing The Winter Game of hanging a few at a time over the stove and hoping to get them all dry before the next wash-day. Al is younger than I, and I thought that with her looks and intelligence and background, she ought to be Outside, seeing life. I couldn't make up my mind whether she really was contented here, or whether it was simply a case of her being old-fashioned enough to believe in whither thou goest.

Then about three years ago, when she was recuperating from an operation in Boston, Mabel Sias and I went to see her. We tried to persuade her to go to New York with us before returning to the woods. I'd just come down from Middle

Dam, and I was able to assure her that Larry was getting along all right; and Mabel had just come up from New York, full of all the wonderful things we could do and see there. We three would have a marvelous time, we told her, and there was no reason in the world why she couldn't go, as soon as the doctor would let her.

She said yes, she knew she'd enjoy it, and yes, she knew Larry would be all right, but—

"But what?" Mabel demanded. "Come on now, Butch, give me one good reason why you can't come."

Al raised her lashes and looked at us squarely with her beautiful eyes, speaking with an almost child-like simplicity and wistfulness. "I know you're going to think I'm silly—but I just want to go home!"

Of course that was the one really good reason for which there was no answer, so we stopped pestering her and gave up the whole notion. But since that day I haven't wasted any more of my time worrying about Al. I haven't felt it necessary.

3

Planned Economy for One

WHENEVER PEOPLE TALK to me about Maine and the back-woods, they seem to expect a hermit, and it so happens that we have one, or a reasonable facsimile thereof. I was a little bit confused about our hermit when first I knew him. This was long before I ever met him, in the days when our acquaintance was confined to telephone conversations. It's true that he's my next-door neighbor on the west, but since he lives five miles down on the other side of the river, with no road and no bridge between us, he might as well have been living on the Azores as far as I was concerned, except for the telephone. This is a single strand of uninsulated wire wandering over the river and through the woods, which makes it more or less possible for us to talk to each other: more when the weather is good and the batteries fairly new, and less when the line is bogged down with snow or fallen fir-tops or the batteries are old and weak.

The first time he called me up he introduced himself as Cliff Wiggin and wanted to know whether it was Monday or Tuesday, since he'd lost track of the days. I told him that it was Tuesday the seventeenth. He asked if I were sure, because if it was Tuesday at all, it must be Tuesday the tenth.

By this time I didn't know myself what the day or date was, although we did agree that the month was October, so I said I'd find out and call him back. By looking at the cover of the last week's *Time*, I determined that it was indeed the seventeenth, and cranked the four long peals that would summon him back to his phone. A voice said, "Wallace speaking," so I asked the voice please to tell Mr. Wiggin that it was Tuesday the seventeenth, and the voice laughed and said that it would. And that took care of that.

During the next two or three months I talked occasionally with Mr. Wallace and occasionally with Mr. Wiggin about the weather, the hunting, and the proper proportions of soda and cream of tartar to use when you ran out of baking powder and wanted to make biscuits. From these exchanges I built up for myself a cozy little picture of those two old cronies holed up in their snug little cabin at the foot of the falls, sharing their tasks and pleasures. Mr. Wiggin apparently was the one who did most of the outdoor work—at least, he mentioned things like banking the house for winter and digging the root crops—and for some reason I thought of him as tall and broad-shouldered, with a full beard. Mr. Wallace did the cooking and inside work—he told me how to make molasses pie and how to bleach flour sacks with lye—and he was round and apple-cheeked. Since everybody in this country plays cribbage, I could just see them on stormy winter evenings, when the wind whooped off the lake and the snow drifted high on their window sills, bent over the cribbage board in the golden light of a kerosene lamp, pegging away like mad, slapping their knees and laughing companionably when either made a killing. It was a very pretty picture indeed. The only trouble with it was that it was completely false. There weren't both Mr. Wiggin and Mr. Wallace. There was just Old Cliff, who lived alone and sometimes called himself by one name and sometimes by the other. He did all the work, both indoors and out, and spent his evenings catching up on his mending, reading, and playing with the cat.

When I found this out from the game warden, Leon Wilson, I called him up to upbraid him. "You've made me look like an awful fool," I said. "Why did you let me go on and on—?"

He laughed. "Wal, I'll tell you, Miz Rich. First-off, I didn't tumble myself. Then I thought I'd see how long it took you to catch on. It got to be kind of a game. You know how 'tis, livin' back here. Don't take a hell of a lot to keep a feller amused."

I know exactly how it was. I myself was becoming pretty adept at the simpler, one-handed forms of entertainment, and if I could have found anybody gullible enough to believe that I was two other people, I'd have played the role to the hilt. So I told him that all was forgiven, and how did he come by two surnames in the first place? That turned out to be a matter very easily explained.

Cliff was born a Wallace, but he was brought up from his orphan babyhood by a family named Wiggin, over around Magalloway Plantation, near the foot of the Peaks of the Diamond. A Wallace he remained, legally, since he was never adopted, but for easy identification with his foster family, he was more often called Cliff Wiggin while he was growing up. He answered to either name, and gave whichever came first to his tongue when asked. Like most of the boys who were born into this country seventy-odd years ago and like many who are born here now, he took to the woods about as soon as he could walk, which is not surprising, since the woods started within a stone's throw of the kitchen door and ended somewhere up around the Arctic Circle. He learned to hunt and to trap and to fish, and had shot his first deer, long before he was in his teens; and not long after, he was guiding parties from the city during the season, and working in the lumber camps during the winter. At sixteen he was a grown man, doing a man's work and carrying a man's responsibility, a thing not unusual in that time and place.

When he was about twenty, he decided to see the world. He'd come in contact with people from the Outside, and he'd heard their talk and observed their ways. These observations led him to the conclusion that he was as smart as they were. Some of the hen-heads he guided owned five-hundred-dollar rifles and leather jackets as soft and pliable as a piece of old cotton waste, and they couldn't run a compass line through an open pasture. A really up-and-coming joker should be able to do all right Out-in-the-States. Besides, he was curious to find out what lay beyond mountain and lake. So he went up to Massachusetts. Here people always speak of down Maine and up Massachusetts-way, and that used to bother me, as by my reckoning anything on the top of the map is up and anything toward the bottom of the map is down. But Cliff explained that to me once out of his large fund of miscellaneous information. It seems that in the old sailing days, the prevailing wind being south-westerly, you sailed down the wind from Boston to Portland and up the wind when you wanted to go back. Cliff didn't sail up to Massachusetts, though. He walked most of the distance, working his way as he went along.

A sport once told me that he had it all figured out that if Cliff had done all the things he claimed to have done in his lifetime, he'd be one hundred and forty-eight years old the coming spring. What he failed to take into consideration was the essential versatility of any frontiersman. Cliff had no trouble in working his way to Massachusetts. He could cook, pitch hay, handle horses, milk, repair almost anything devised by man, and turn his hand to any one of the scores of other skills included in the liberal education of a pioneer life. He hadn't decided exactly where he was heading, except that it was somewhere far away and exciting. He thought that he'd keep an open mind, take one step at a time, and hold himself ready to recognize and grasp opportunities. This plan, he felt, would lead him to wealth and adventure.

Probably it would have, too, if he hadn't fallen in love shortly after reaching Massachusetts. No Casanova, he found a good steady job in a factory, established himself as a sober, solid citizen and good provider, and armed with these sterling qualifications, wooed and won the girl of his dreams. This should have been the end of the story, and for about twenty-five years it seemed as though it might be. He worked hard and saved his money. He received promotions and raises with encouraging regularity. He bought a house with hardwood floors in every room and a half-acre lot around it. It began to look as though this were just another Horatio Alger story of rags to riches.

Then something happened. Perhaps he woke one night and heard the faint, sweet, discordant cry of the wild geese going over, beating their way northward through the rare, pure altitudes with the moonlight on their backs. Perhaps, walking down the crowded street, he caught a pungent whiff of the alien scent of cut pine, from a building under construction. Perhaps it was nothing more than a dandelion blooming bravely on a starved plot of city grass. Whatever it was, it brought Cliff up short. He asked himself, as we all must do at one time or another, "What in tarnation am I doing here?" This wasn't where he belonged. This wasn't any place he'd ever intended to be, or any life he'd ever intended to live. He realized with surprise and an overwhelming sense of dismay that half his days had been spent, and that middle age found him possessed of nothing that he really wanted. It never occurred to him that he had passed the point of no return.

He wrote a letter to his wife, handing over to her the mortgage-free house and the very respectable bank account, told the boss that he was quitting as of that moment, went down to the station, bought a ticket, got on the train, and came home. It didn't take so very much longer to do than it does to tell about it, and while this course may seem to have been a little ruthless, you can't make an angel cake without smashing a lot of eggs and maybe even throwing away some of the yolks. How his wife took this cavalier treatment, I have no way of knowing for certain. Since Cliff never heard a word from her from that day to this—and he wouldn't have been hard to trace, returning as he did to the green pastures of his youth—I accept his opinion that she didn't really mind having him go.

"I was just a bad habit she'd got into," he explained. "She was used to having me around, just like you get used to a window that jams. Must have been a relief to her, after a while, not havin' me trackin' up her clean floors. I ain't none of these here indispensable men; never was, nor ever aim to be."

When at last he stood again in the shadow of the Peaks, he had no money and only the clothes that he stood in, but this didn't worry him. He figured that he was almost exactly as well off as he had been on that day a quarter of a century before, when he had set out to see the world. True, he had lost twenty-five years and the physical qualities of youth; but he had gained something of greater value, something a surprising number of people never acquire. He knew now exactly what he wanted from life. He wanted peace and freedom, and he intended to have them. He knew what he was about. He realized that peace and freedom are almost incompatible: that if you want freeom, you'll almost surely have to fight for it, but if you'd rather have peace, you can probably have it by selling yourself into some form of bondage. Well, he was prepared to do a little fighting when necessary—he'd already fought and won the Battle of Massachusetts; and he was prepared to accept a few temporary bonds while he was establishing the conditions under which he would, by his own definition, feel free and at peace. The thing that worried him most was time. He'd frittered away half his life, and he didn't intend to waste the other half.

He could have gone back to what he had been, an itinerant woodsman and guide, but there was no future in that, and not much of a present. The thing for him to do, he decided, was to acquire a fishing and hunting camp and set himself up in the sports business. Thus he'd have a home of his own and a source of the small income he needed for his very few wants. He'd be his own boss, and he'd be what he called "shed of folks." He'd had enough bosses, and folks crowding in on him, during the past twenty-five years to last him the rest of his life.

He cruised about the country, familiar from old time, and finally located a set—as we say in Maine—of run-down camps, so far gone that he was able to lease them very cheaply. There was a four-room cabin with a pitch-roofed loft, outhouses, an icehouse, and a woodshed. The roofs leaked like sieves, the floor of the porch was rotted away, some of the windows were broken, porcupines had been at the thresholds, and there was no plumbing of any description. But the sills and timbers were sound, there was a good place for a garden, once it was cleared of encroaching brush and grubbed free of roots, and plenty of hardwood for fuel stood within easy hauling distance. The site was as perfect as possible in a world of imperfections. The buildings were on a tongue of land running out between Lake Umbagog and the river, with water on three sides of it. At the back, the deep sheltered reach of the river offered perfect anchorage for boats, and the view from the porch across the open lake to the mountains of New Hampshire was superb. Every breeze that blew crossed the point, and on the hottest day it was cool there. The territory offered excellent hunting, and the fishing was good and varied—trolling on the lake or fly-fishing in the five miles of river pools behind. Perhaps best of all, no road or trail led within miles of the place. It was exactly what Cliff wanted.

So he went to work for somebody else in the woods long enough to earn money for a year's rental and a modest grubstake, and moved in. There was plenty of work on the buildings that he could do alone to keep him busy for a long time; but he soon realized that he was going to need more money than he had estimated. The cost of lumber and building materials had risen fantastically on account of the war—the first World War, that was. The place was in no condition as yet for paying guests. Cliff could have gone back to work in the woods, or more profitable still, in a war plant; but he thought it was too dangerous, even for a short time. "You climb a little way out on a limb, and first thing off the pickle boat, you find yourself in a bear trap," he said, with a fine free mixing of metaphors. "I done that once, and look at the mess I got into. I warn't takin' no more chances. Not me. I'd finally got back to home base, and I made up my mind I was goin' to hang snug, if I had to live off potatoes and salt."

Just about then, when the potatoes and salt appeared to be developing into more than a manner of speaking, National Prohibition became a fact. Now the rural districts of Maine have always been, and probably always will be, peopled by a fairly large body of inspired and two-fisted drinkers. I suppose this is true, possibly, of most places where the work is back-breaking and monotonous, and the opportunities for recreation few and far between. Maine, moreover, had been a temperance state ever since it was a state at all, and the citizens from the backwoods, who stayed at home and minded their own affairs, had always nursed a dark suspicion that State Prohibition was a burden that had been foisted on them when their backs were turned by smart-aleck legislators down in 'Gusta. The injustice of this charge is beside the point. The point is that drinking was more than an escape or a pleasure; it came pretty near to being a duty of the right-minded.

Now it became apparent that the day was about to dawn when passable drinking liquor was going to be even harder-come-by than ever. The close proximity of the Canadian Border made it inevitable that a surprising number of upright citizens should decide that smuggling wasn't really a crime, especially if you didn't get caught. On the nights of the dark of the moon, the narrow little secret trails across ridges and along hidden valleys knew well the silent footsteps of shadowy men who shouldered heavy pack-sacks which they handled like crates of eggs. The trouble with that liquor was that it was expensive—definitely not the poor man's potion. The poor man could resort to the lumberjack special, canned heat, or he could hunt up a farmer with a full silo, and persuade him to tap it and drain off the juice at the bottom. Neither of these drinks was very expensive initially, but the consequences of drinking them might be before long, providing you could choke them down at all. They were never palatable, and they were often lethal.

It occurred to Cliff that what this neck of the woods needed was a safe, not too costly, drinkable liquor, and that by the long arm of Providence, he was the man to provide it. Years before he had guided the vice-president of a famous old distillery, and one night over the campfire the man had talked shop to him. He'd told how rum was made, growing almost poetic about it, as men who are absorbed in their work will do. He'd been eloquent enough so that Cliff, who is like a magpie when it comes to collecting and storing away miscellaneous and glittering, although possibly useless, bits of information, remembered the formula and process. It was the famous one, the one which contributed so largely to New England commerce and wealth in the old, bad, swashbuckling molasses-slave-and-rum trading days. Cliff decided that it might as well contribute to his wealth, too.

He knew the perfect place to conduct his new enterprise, over in the deep woods by Sunday Brook. There he had everything he needed, a steady flow of icy water, plenty of fuel, and complete privacy. He could get over there by boat and trail in three-quarters of an hour, and nobody the wiser. So he bought some barrels of black molasses, set up a hay-wire, or homemade, still, and went into production. Larry Parsons once told me that Cliff made wonderful rum, smooth, dark, and powerful, and that he didn't charge half enough for it. "He could have cleaned up a fortune," Larry told me, "but you know how Cliff is. You can't tell him anything, once he's got his mind made up. He figured on making a fair profit, and that's all he'd take. Not that anybody tried very hard to talk him into doubling his prices. If he wanted to play Santa Claus, nobody was going to stop him." Larry laughed reminiscently. "You know what the old joker did? He even gave a rebate if you brought back the empty jug."

I truly believe that this fair-trade policy was dictated by honesty, and that just goes to show that honesty is really the best policy after all. Not only did the good word quickly get around, so that the drinking world started beating a track to Cliff's door, but all of his customers were so grateful and well satisfied that they took the greatest pains to do nothing that would involve him in the toils of the law. In a surprisingly short time he was making money hand over fist, and he could have made a lot more, if he'd been reasonable.

His unreasonableness lay in his refusal to increase the volume of production. As he viewed it, things were all right just as they stood. He wasn't in the moonshine business. His real business was getting his sporting camp into running order, and the still was a small, though necessary, side line, unimportant except that it enabled him to buy kegs of nails, matched siding, and other necessities. He didn't want to spend too much time running off his rum. He had too much work to do at home, important work like painting and setting glass and clearing up his garden plot. He didn't mind taking his boat over to Sunday Cove two-three times a week. It was a pretty ride and sometimes he caught a fish or found a useful piece of flotsam or jetsam, such as a cantdog, lost on the drive, or a good sound piece of eight-by-eight off one of the dams. He could mull things over during the boat ride. The drone of the outboard and the sight of the familiar shore sliding by were conducive to clear thinking, and the solution to such problems as how to place a new sill under the kitchen single-handed without wrecking the place swam easily to the top of his mind. He didn't object to the walk up Sunday Brook to the still, as long as he didn't have to take it too often. There were blueberries and raspberries to be picked in season as he went along, and in the fall he could take his gun and knock off a partridge or two for a stew, or get a shot at a deer. Later he took a few traps along and put in some mink and beaver sets, as much for fun as for the cash the pelts would bring. It was all pleasant enough, but he wasn't going to be diverted from his primary object of getting his camp into shape by tying himself down to another still. It was pointed out to him that by enlarging his business he could make enough money to hire half a dozen carpenters to help him, if he wanted to, but he dismissed this idea as the purest folly.

"What would I want with a mess of carpenters diddling 'round doin' everything wrong the minute my back was turned? If you want a dog hung right, hang him yourself, I always say. Top of that, they'd be expectin' their meals on time. I might just as well be back punchin' a time-clock in the factory as tied down to a cook-stove. Me, I eat when I get hungry. And s'posin' I'd get hung up some place—wound a deer, say, and have to track it all day—and didn't get home when they expected me. They'd be a-worryin' and a-frettin' and a-gettin' out a posse after me. One thing I can't abide, it's knowin' someone's home stewin' about me. Takes all the pleasure out of life. Then take evenin's. They'd want to be jawrin' and yarnin', and sometimes a man don't want his ears all hacked up with a lot of foolish talk. Might just as well be married again as shacked up with a gang of carpenters. Nope, I aim to keep on the way I am, and what folks don't like, they can lump."

That was that.

But the money kept coming in and the time arrived when Cliff decided that he had all he needed. His camps were now in good repair, with tight roofs and firm foundations. He'd bought a new boat to replace the old wreck he'd been using, and he had material on hand for a new float and boathouse. He'd bought simple but adequate furnishings for the camp, and there was no object in wasting any more time fooling around. Spring was just around the corner, and he wanted to open up for business as soon as the ice went out. He had yet to get the last of his wood under cover and do his spring cleaning. After that there'd be his garden to plant and his sports to look after. He'd be a very busy man.

So one morning he arose very early, while it was still pitch dark. He took a look at the thermometer and the sky and decided that if he started at once, he'd be back before the sun had risen high enough to soften the crust. It had thawed the day before, but after sunset the mercury had plunged down nearly to zero. So this morning conditions were ideal for hauling a heavy sled, and the Lord only knew when they'd be so again. He put on his creepers, got the sled out of the lean-to, put a box of necessary tools aboard it, and set out for Sunday Brook. The going was good. His creepers bit crisply into the crust, and the sled followed easily, its runners squeaking and whispering on the snow, a low accompaniment to his tuneless whistling. His breath streamed like a white scarf over his shoulder, freezing on his parka hood, but his blood coursed warm and vigorous through his veins, and he felt wonderful. This was a great day, he thought as he strode along, watching the familiar pine- and spruce-tops along the shore emerge from night against the graying eastern sky. This was the last time he'd be taking this trip for a long while to come, perhaps forever, unless he felt like dropping over this way sometimes in the fall, deer hunting. Well, he was glad to be shed of the business, although in all fairness it had served him a good turn. He couldn't rightly say otherwise.

He was at work before the sun was up, dismantling the still, pausing now and then to blow on his fingers or thrust his hands into the warmth of his armpits. Handling the icy metal and tools was a cold business. He'd heard and read about Government agents smashing stills, and he thought maybe it would be more fitting if he did the same, just to show he was through. It would be kind of dramatic and give him a lot of satisfaction for a few minutes, but it wasn't a very sensible thing to do—not when so much of the stuff was perfectly good and would come in awful handy around the camp. He loaded the sled with salvaged parts, dug up a few gallons of rum he'd cached under a snowdrift and added them to the pile, lashed his load secure, and started out for home.

The sun was up, gilding the tops of the trees on the other side of the cove, and he'd have to hurry if he didn't want to end up floundering hip-deep in wet snow. The downhill run through the woods to the shore was easy, but when he started along the level of the lake, the sled began to hang back. He stuffed his mittens under the ropes where they dragged on his shoulders, to ease the bite, and plodded on. To-morrow, he thought, maybe, if the weather held good and he felt like it, he'd try to get over the mountain to Magalloway and start the word going that he wasn't making no more rum. After he'd sold this piddling little eight-ten gallons, he was through. No need of inconveniencing folks to come clean into his place for nothing. No need of inconveniencing himself, either, having them interrupting his work.

It wasn't quite as simple as all that, though. To his surprise and indignation—because what he did was his own business, he considered—his clients put up what he termed an awful holler. "They come cryin' 'round, beggin' and pleadin' with me. 'Ain't no use your arguin',' I told them. 'Might as well save your breath. I don't cal'late to make no more liquor. Don't drink myself, and don't hold with drinkin'. Wine is a mocker,' I said. Didn't mean to put it on so thick, but they was all dingin' at me, and I lost my temper. Don't see no harm in the other feller's takin' a drink, if he's so minded, so long as he don't try to make me go agin my principles. But there warn't no need to get nasty like some of them jokers did, sayin' I was a good one to preach after runnin' a still all that time. Like I told them, that warn't law-breakin'. That was necessity. Now that 'twarn't necessary no longer, I didn't aim to go breakin' the law. 'You can have what liquor I got here,' I told them, 'at the reg'lar price, but when it's gone, there ain't no more.' Couldn't seem to get it through their thick heads. They kept tellin' me I was crazy, passin' up an easy livin' like that. What did I want with an easy livin' and money in the bank? Had money in the bank once, I told them. Plenty of it, too, and what good did it do me? 'Nope,' I told them, 'you might as well make up your minds to it and quit pesterin' me. I got things to do and no time to waste.' "

Finally he managed to convince them that he meant what he said. It was a tough fight, but I guess it was worth it. More than thirty years have elapsed since, and during that time no one has tried to argue Cliff into or out of anything, once he has announced his attitude and intentions.

I saw Cliff for the first time about twelve years ago. Of course we'd been carrying on over the telephone for five years or so before that. We'd swapped recipes, local gossip, home remedies, and advice. We'd joined in cursing dog-days and the Wright brothers, whose irresponsible antics were going to end in ruining the lakes and any chance of privacy a man might have left to him. The occasion for this was when nobody had been able to get Cliff on the telephone for five days. It was in the middle of winter, and he was living alone, of course. In this country when anyone lives alone and off the beaten track, the neighbors—the term is loose; a neighbor is the nearest person, be he one or twenty miles away—try to keep a casual check on him. It's easy to break a leg or contract double pneumonia in the woods, and if you're alone, either can be disastrous. I'd tried to call Cliff a couple of times myself with no success, and so, apparently, had Joe Mooney at the Brown Farm. Joe called me one evening and wanted to know when I'd last talked with Cliff. It had been several days before.

"Maybe his line's out of order," I suggested.

"Maybe," Joe said, "but I don't think so. It was all right last Sunday, and we haven't had any snow or high winds since. Nobody else's line is down. We'll give him one more try. Help me ring, will you, Louise?" Helping anyone ring probably needs some explanation, since I'm sure it's a custom peculiar to lines like ours. When the batteries are weak or the lines are wet, you can crank your arm off, but the result at the other end may be nothing louder than a faint tinkle. However, if two people ring together on different phones, it boosts the decibels—or whatever else you call it—and a quite respectable clangor issues from the third. This night, however, Joe and I rang in concert for ten minutes, and nothing happened.

"Well, I dunno," Joe said at last from his post fifteen miles away over the mountain. "Seems like that ought to have waked the dead. Guess we'll send a plane In in the morning, just to be sure he's all right. A plane ought to be able to land on the ice, hadn't it?"

I said I thought so, if you could judge Umbagog by the Richardsons. The snow was deep, but it was packed hard and smooth, and if the pilot got In early, before it softened up enough to cake on his skis, he shouldn't have any trouble. So the next morning at about six o'clock, when it was barely light, I hear the drone of a motor high in the air over Umbagog-way.

At noon Cliff called me up. I was glad to hear his voice sounding hale and hearty, but he didn't seem any too pleased to hear mine. "They claim you and Joe been worryin' about me," he accused.

"Yes, we have," I said. "Where've you been? I've tried and tried to get you."

"I been right here where I belong."

"Have you been sick?"

"Nope, never better in my life. I been busy."

"Well, then why couldn't we get you? Was your line down?"

"Nope. Oh, I heard it a-clatterin' away all right, off and on all week, but I didn't feel like answerin' it. Didn't feel like talkin' to nobody, so I let the damn thing ring. Then that flyin' fool comes bargin' In, right when I'm gettin' my feet braced to overhaul my saw rig. I sure gave him his go-on-home-a-cryin'. Seems like a man can't have no peace a-tall 'round here no more."

And that's how we happened to be condemning the Wright brothers; because Cliff prophesied darkly that it wasn't going to end with a joker's having his breakfast hour all shot to hell. Next thing they'd be running regular taxi services In to the lakes, to ruin the fishing and scare the bejesus out of the game, and how would I like that? I said meekly that I wouldn't like it at all. He informed me that furthermore he wouldn't stand for havin' folks a-worryin' and a-frettin' about him, because it made him as oneasy as a cat. He hung up with finality.

Eventually Ralph and I acquired a boat down on Umbagog, and so widened our field of action to include Cliff's bailiwick. We were slatting down the lake one day when he appeared on his dock and waved us in. He wanted to know whether I wanted some rhubarb to stew up. He had all kinds of it, he said, and I was welcome to as much as I cared to pull. He looked, I am happy to report, exactly as I had finally made up my mind that he should—tall, lanky, ageless, and durable. After I'd picked my rhubarb and admired his garden and tame rabbits, we inspected the new peeled-log bunkhouse he was building so that he could accommodate a few more sports.

"I ain't makin' it too big," he said. "Just big enough. I don't aim to have no more sports than I can cook for myself without bustin' a gut. Minute you start hirin' people to work for you, you stop bein' boss. I aim to be boss."

We sat on the porch for a while, drinking tea and taking turns looking through his spyglass at passing boats on the lake. It was a real spyglass, the single-barreled kind that you can stretch out to a length of two feet, and Cliff kept it on the porch, he said, so that he could identify approaching craft and decide at his leisure whether he wanted to bother with the occupants, or whether he'd rather go hide in the bush until they were gone. Life was too short to waste any of it on fools, and while he was hiding in the woods, he could be improving his time in any number of ways. Then he rose to his feet and said he'd better be getting at his chores. I'd heard about Cliff's methods, so I knew we'd better be going.

The three of us walked down to the dock together along the narrow little grass-grown path in the pleasant shade of the few big birches he'd left standing for beauty's sake, and all the time I was wondering whether I dared to offer to bring down some horse-radish roots for him to heel in, the next time we went by. I was afraid he might think I was being forward. He'd gone to quite a lot of trouble to eliminate social contacts from his life, and I cherish privacy too much myself to risk infringing upon another's right to it. My broodings and soul searchings were interrupted by the approach of a kicker-boat around the point from the lake.

In the stern was Ben Bennett, an old guide whom we all knew, with two sports in the center and bow seats. We knew they were sports because they had on beautiful Pendleton shirts, high waders, and life belts. Ben throttled his motor down and drew alongside. He wanted to know, he said, if he could borrow a couple of shear pins. He didn't have a spare, and he aimed to go up the river to fish. He didn't cal'late to hit any rocks, but in that river you never could tell, and if he sheared a pin, he sure as hell didn't aim to row all the way back to Chandler's. Cliff said he didn't blame him a mite, and started searching under the seat of his own kicker-boat, drawn up on the float, for the ditty-box in which he kept his spare parts. In the meantime the sports began making conversation.

"It seems impossible to believe that there are places like this," one said enthusiastically. "It does a man good to get away once in a while, to live close to Nature, to forget his worries. Why, I'm a new man since I've been up here." He leaned forward, carried away, and Ben prudently shifted his weight to trim the boat. "Do you realize," the sport went on impressively, "do you *realize* that it's been eight days since we've heard the whistle of a train?" He leaned back expectantly, and we were saved the necessity of replying as Cliff found the shear pins, thrust them into Ben's hand, and shoved the boat off with scant ceremony. We watched them recede up the river.

Then Cliff blew out his breath. "Wal, now, ain't he the little wonder of the ages?" he demanded. "Ain't he the copper-riveted modern marvel? Eight whole days he ain't heard a train a-whistlin'." He turned to me. "When'd you hear your last train, Miz Rich?"

I did a little rapid thinking back. "Let's see. About four and a half years ago, as nearly as I can remember; and if it's another four and a half years to come, that'll still be too soon."

"Barrin' one time I was down to Berlin ten years ago, I ain't heard one myself for well nigh onto sixteen years. Used to hear them all night long when I was livin' up in Massachusetts. If there's a more Godforsaken sound, I don't know about it."

"I don't either," I agreed wholeheartedly. "People who visit us get the shivers when they hear a loon, they say it's so eerie—"

"Or a lynx yowlin' back on the ridge in the night," he took up the tale. "Or geese honkin' over. Why, them's all real home-like sounds, comfortable and natural as broke-in boots." He stopped and changed the subject abruptly. "Come see me again. Drop in any time. Door ain't never locked, in case I ain't around."

"Thank you," I said, genuinely pleased. "We will. I'll bring you down some horse-radish roots, if you want them." He said he did, and after that we did call on him occasionally, but not often enough to wear out our welcome. He only came to see us once, and that was only because he was guiding a sport who wanted to meet an author. Cliff was self-admittedly not much of a hand for visitin' 'round. On this occasion he did the honors punctiliously, but as soon as he decently could, he oozed out the door and spent the rest of the call inspecting the V-belt arrangement on the saw rig, with the idea of rebuilding his own. In that way he could figure that the visit hadn't been a total waste of time.

The last time I saw Cliff was down at Errol Dam, the western gate to the lake region from the Outside. He was unloading four rather puzzled- and disgruntled-looking men from his boat onto the landing, tossing their duffle out after them with a fine no-nonsense-now air. After they had climbed into their cars and gone away, he lowered his boat down the current alongside ours, so we could pass the time of day.

"I thought that party was going to stay until the end of the week," I remarked, "and here it is only Wednesday. What happened? Did they get called home?"

He spat into the water and started winding his motor cord. "Nope."

"Didn't they like your place?"

"Yep, liked it fine. But I'll tell you how it was, Miz Rich. I got sick an' tired of hearin' them gab, so this mornin' I told them to pack up their gear, I didn't want them 'round under foot any more. An' they did."

"Why, Cliff!" I exclaimed, horrified. "You're in business! You can't do a thing like that."

"Wal, mebbe not, but I done it. I ain't beholden to them nor to nobody. 'Tain't worth the twenty dollars a day to me to put up with their clatter. Got up this mornin' with a notion I'd like to go trollin' in the Deep Hole, an' I'd like to go alone. An' by the great horn spoon, that's what I'm a-goin' to do."

He yanked on the cord of the outboard, and it roared into life. He lifted his hand in casual salute and started off up the river, an old, shabby, lonely figure, looking very small in his little boat on the wide waters between the somnolent summer shores—but for all that, the figure of a free man.

4

Paid Notice

IN THIS COUNTRY, so sparsely settled and so little traveled, you often hear for years about people without ever having seen them. You know their names and their characters and how they're getting on in the world, and finally you feel as though you were acquainted with them, and you develop a true interest in them. We have so little to amuse us here—no plays, no movies, no concerts—that we have to extract what drama we can out of the life around us. Our chief diversion is talking, and what is there more interesting to talk about than people? I suppose this comes under the heading of gossip, and I must admit that much of the talk is unkind and destructive. But this is not, I believe, so much because the majority of people wish ill to others as because exaggerated tales of double-dealing and misfortune and villainy are in themselves more exciting than accurate reports of the doings of the God-fearing and hard-working. However that may be, all I knew for a long time about Jones Corners and the Crews I got second-hand from Catherine Jacobs, who once lived over around there. Catherine worked for me for four years during the war, and in the course of four years under the same roof we managed to cover quite a bit of territory, orally, neither one of us being exactly a strong silent type.

I don't know why, of all the people in Jones Corners that Catherine talked about, I became especially interested in the career of the Crews, since here, certainly, was a family about whom nothing scandalous or derogatory could be said. They were decent and self-respecting, and they worked like dogs to make a living off their poor little farm. Perhaps the reason that I sympathized with Betty Crew was that I too had once been a schoolteacher from Away, and that I too knew what it was to be poor and to work hard. I knew what it meant to come from a life made easy by modern plumbing and electric lights to a life complicated by kerosene lamp chimneys to be washed every day and a balky pump, with hot water something to be hoarded, since every drop had to be heated on the top of a wood-burning kitchen range. So although I had never laid eyes on the woman in my life, I was always glad to hear news of Betty Crew of Jones Corners.

The place hasn't changed much in the thirty years since Betty Freeman went there, fresh out of Normal School, to teach in the little three-room school. It was then the tiny civic center of a scattered farming community, and it still is. The main road through the village has been hard-surfaced since then, and what used to be the blacksmith's shop now has a gas pump out in front and a free air hose hung up beside the wide door. Perhaps some of the half dozen houses clustered around the cross-roads wear a newer coat of paint, and surely the lilac bushes and rambler roses have grown taller and rambled further; but these are the only visible signs of change. The stone Union soldier still presents arms tirelessly upon his pedestal in the grassy enclosure where the roads cross; the harsh-toned bell of the white church still sends out its summons through the Sunday morning air; and the citizens of the town still assemble in the combined General Store and Post Office at four in the afternoon, when the mail stage is due. Very few of them expect mail, but the arrival of the stage is a good excuse to drop work and go down to the store to pick up the news and trade in their butter and eggs for sugar and tea.

The chief difference between the Jones Corners of fifty or seventy-five years ago and the Jones Corners of to-day is that then it had a future and now you might almost say that it hasn't even a past. The bright dreams of the settlers never materialized. It never grew beyond its early stages. The world simply went another way and left it, as it has so many northern New England towns, little more than a survival. The same buildings stand; the same customs and attitudes are adhered to; descendants of the same families farm the same grudging fields that their forebears wrested from the forest. If anything, the place has retrogressed. Some of the family names current fifty years ago exist now only on the dim slate markers in the village cemetery. The descendants of many buried there have gone away, defeated by the stubborn Maine soil and the ruthless Maine climate. The second growth has taken back their fields, the heaving frost has overthrown their boundary walls, and time and neglect have leveled their buildings. It's not much of a loss. They weren't very good farms anyway, just marginal land from which only those more stubborn and ruthless than soil and climate could possibly make a living—people like the Bennetts and the Bartletts, the Hodges and the Abbotts, the Hazens and the Crews.

It was a Crew whom Betty married after her second year

of teaching: Bert, the last of the family and sole heir to the stony, up-ended, impoverished Crew acres and the shabby old Crew homestead, stuck away on a dirt road three miles from the center. Everybody in town said that Bert was making a terrible mistake. The schoolteacher didn't know anything about hard work, and all she'd do would be fritter away Bert's money on foolishness, and, in the end, probably leave him. He'd do better to stick to his own kind, they said; there were plenty of girls around town who'd be more than willing. And I guess that was true, because Bert was likeable and dependable and attractive, in an unspectacular, slow-spoken way. As for Betty's friends, they thought she was just plain crazy to bury herself for the rest of her life way back in the sticks. She'd be miserable, they said; and it wasn't as if there were any hope of influencing Bert to move somewhere else. That was true, too. The farm was his home and the home of his forefathers, and he took a wordless pride in hanging onto it. He had roots going down into the thin soil of the Crew land far deeper probably than he himself realized. It would be easier to move the granite ledge back of the barn to another location than it would be to move Bert Crew off the Crew farm.

Betty didn't care what anybody said. She loved Bert and he loved her, and that was all that mattered. She was going into this thing with her eyes open. She'd lived in the community for two years, she'd seen what being a farmer's wife meant, and she was prepared to be one. Given time, she was sure that she could correct all the wrong impressions about her.

And she did. Off the beaten track though the Crew place was, before the summer was over every woman in town had found or made occasion to call on Betty Crew. How casual callers could know about the absence of dust from the tops of the picture frames or the state of their hostess' bureau drawers I wouldn't be in a position to say; but know they did, and the reports brought back were favorable. Betty was said to be a good housekeeper. She put out a nice white wash, too, and I, who know, tell you that that is quite a feat when you have no washing machine and have to heat the water on the stove in an old copper boiler. In the time between Bert's mother's death and his marriage to Betty, the rule that a patch is no disgrace but a hole is a scandal had been in abeyance. After all, Bert was trying to run the farm and do his own cooking, housework, and laundry, so he deserved a little leni-ence. But now it came back into operation again, full force. The first time after the wedding that Bert showed up at the store, every woman in the place maneuvered herself into a position behind him from which she could study the patch on the shoulder of his faded blue shirt. It was a work of art, with the edges turned neatly under and the stitches tiny and even. When he told Sam Abbott to stop saving him a loaf of bread every other day and bought yeast instead, heads were nodded in approval. Only slatterns allowed boughten bread on their tables—sleazy stuff with no body to it that won't stand by a man any time at all. Self-respecting housewives make their own honest bread. Then in the fall Betty turned her old winter coat and dyed it, instead of buying a new one; and from then on she was less and less criticized, until in a surprisingly short time she was accepted.

"How do you mean, a short time?" I asked Catherine, when she told me that. I'd had some experience myself in storming the local citadels.

"Oh, seven or eight years. No time at all, really."

I said, "You mean her troubles were over? Nobody talked about her any more? She lived happily ever after?"

Catherine snorted. "Of course not. Nobody lives happily ever after. Where there's life, there's always something to worry over and something to criticize. You know how people are. And besides, by that time she had the twins, Freeman and Carolyn, and whenever there was nothing else to talk about, the old hens would start ripping into Betty for the way she spoiled Carolyn."

"Well, did she spoil Carolyn, really?" I asked.

"I don't know, Louise. It would be hard to say. Maybe she did and maybe she didn't. If she did, I don't know that I blame her much. Carolyn was the cutest kid you ever laid eyes on, the kind it would be awful hard not to spoil. She was fair like her mother, though of course Betty's faded a lot now. But Carolyn's hair was the only really gold hair I ever saw in my life, and it curled all over her head like a halo. She had the sweetest little face. She had a sweet nature, too, so sunny and obliging and sort of *giving*. Freeman took after his father, and you'd never know those children were twins. He was dark and serious and thoughtful, and I think he was the *best* child—you know how some children are just *born* good?"

I said no, I didn't know. In my experience, every child was capable of devilishness, my own not excepted.

"Well, you ought to have known Freeman Crew. If ever a child was a little angel—"

I said, probably inspired by jealousy, that he sounded like a smug piece to me, too good to be true, or else a little lacking.

"No, really, he wasn't like that. He was bright—both kids were bright as buttons—and full of fun, but he was just *good*.

I don't mean that Carolyn was *bad*. It was just that she was a born tumble-heels, the way some people are. If one of them fell into a brook or out of a tree, it was always Carolyn. If a glass of milk got tipped over at table, it had to be Carolyn's. Look, I took care of them once for two-three days, when Betty's mother died and she had to go down-country to the funeral, and I'll tell you how it was—"

This is how it was. For all she had been prepared for, and accepted readily and without mental reservations, the life she'd married into, Betty did find the existence on the farm bleak and austere. Perhaps she herself didn't realize it. She took pride in her increasing competence and derived a great deal of satisfaction from her own and Bert's accomplishments, and found reward in Bert's love and admiration. Still it was a pretty Spartan life, stripped of the small extras over and above the necessities, the silly little things that make living fun. She didn't go much of anywhere, partly because at the end of the day she was too tired to make the effort required to change her clothes and drive over the rough road to the village to attend Church Suppers and meetings of the Grange, getting back late to a shortened night's sleep; and partly because, whether she would admit it or not, she found it depressing always to be one of the less-well-dressed women there, always to hear about some other housewife's having acquired a new linoleum or a water-heater, while she was making-do with what she had. She wasn't envious and she didn't complain; but there it was, all the same.

Then, after all this time of putting up with second-bests, the twins were born, and at last she and Bert had something a little bit finer than anyone else in town had. There is something special about twins, and these were such beautiful babies. It was no wonder that she and Bert took delight in them. Delight—that's the word: great pleasure, joyful satisfaction. Those were the things that had been lacking from the farm, and as the twins grew a little older and could follow their mother and father around on eager, uncertain feet, those were the things that came to the Crews in ever-increasing measure.

Now feeding the poultry became a pleasure instead of a routine chore, because the twins were there—Carolyn toddling shrieking into the flock, trying to catch a pullet to cuddle, while Freeman squatted on his heels as still as a little stone, holding out a handful of grain until he had lured one under his hand. The big old trout that had been caught and put into the well by Bert's father, to keep the water pure, was remembered again after many years and given a name, Mr. Higgins; and it became a game to try to see him as he hung, self-sufficient and supercilious, in the icy depths at the bottom of the fern-fringed stone-lined shaft. Freeman often saw him, for he learned quickly that the greatest care must be taken not to startle Mr. Higgins. He would inch his dark little head over the coping by imperceptible degrees, and there the great fish would be. But when he called Carolyn, she would run up laughing and thrust her shining head over the opening—and there would be nothing to see at all except the two faces, the one so dark and grave, the other so fair and gay, reflected far below against the blue reflected sky, in a frame of dripping stonework and greenery. Everything on the farm took on new meaning and significance with the coming of the twins, and even Bert, who had lived there all his life and loved the place to his very bones, found new things to marvel at and rejoice in almost daily. For the first time since he could remember, he discovered himself standing and staring at an apple tree in bloom, seeing it not in terms of possible bushels of saleable fruit, but as the children saw it, a miracle of transitory loveliness, its own excuse for fragrant being.

Then the twins were old enough to go to school, and the horizons of the farm broadened. Because they were so quick and eager and intelligent, from the very first they were included in all the little school programs. The teacher knew that when The Day came, Freeman and Carolyn would be line-perfect and immaculate in the beautiful clothes that Betty made them out of the hand-me-downs which her city sister, unseen now for years and virtually lost to her, sent to the farm. That was when the criticism started. "The way she dresses that child! You'd think she was Somebody!" and "Takes the clothes right off her own back," and "I only hope she don't live to regret it." But Bert and Betty, sitting in the audience in their shabby decent wear, looking and listening with all their eyes and ears to the charming—and it almost seemed sometimes charmed—pair on the platform, were unconscious of comment. Freeman would stand there as serious and responsible as a little judge; but Carolyn's eyes would seek out her parents, and then her whole face would break into a smile that carried her entire heart with it. Betty's gaze would meet Bert's shyly, seeking confirmation of the incredible fact that these were indeed their very own. ("Look at the way they smirk at those young-ones, like they were little tin gods!" and "There is such a thing as making a fool of yourself over your children.")

Perhaps Betty was wrong. Perhaps she should have punished Carolyn more often—"Spare the rod, I always say"—for the childish disasters into which her impetuous spirit so often impelled her. But she believed that she knew her daughter, and that she was one to be driven with a light rein.

The twins were graduated with honors from the Jones Corners Grammar School, and went, along with the rest of their classmates, to the High School in the nearest large town. They were both immediately popular, and that's not so easy for a "bussy," a transported pupil whose schoolday starts with the ringing of the eight forty-five bell and ends promptly with the one-thirty dismissal gong, when the buses are champing to be gone, leaving no time for extracurricular activities or the cultivation of new friends.

"I know," said Catherine to me. "I was a bussy once myself and it's a tough life. You just never get to know any of the other pupils, except the kids from your own town, and you knew them anyhow. But Carolyn and Freeman do all right. He plays on all the teams and Tim Bartlett has taken to beauing her around. He lives at the Corners, a couple of miles back from the Crews. The kids have known each other all their lives, but you know how it is. He never paid her much mind until he saw how the other new boys flocked around her. They're really awfully cute together. They're simply crazy over each other, kid-fashion."

"What does her mother think about it?" I asked.

"Oh, I guess she doesn't take it very seriously. She has ideas about the twins. She's planning to send them to college somehow."

But it wasn't to work out that way.

Immediately after graduation, when he was barely seventeen, Freeman came home one day and announced that he had decided to enlist. He needed his parents' permission, he said; but if they wouldn't give it, he'd just run away and lie about his age. His reason was typical of him: "I've decided I ought to."

His mother wrung her hands, literally. That's a phrase I've read often, and in print it sounds very false and melodramatic. But have you ever seen anyone do it? It's the most pitiful gesture in the world, especially when it is used by a woman like Betty Crew, who has depended on her hands to meet all the crises of her adult life, and who is confronted with a situation where all the strength and patience and skill and tenderness of her ten fingers and roughened palms can be of no avail. Here is my defense against the world, the gesture seems to say, rendered invalid. "But, Freeman," she said, "why? Can't you wait for the draft? You won't like that kind of life. It may sound very exciting and adventurous, but it won't be. You'll hate being crowded into barracks. You've always had your own room and done as you chose—"

"I know it," said Freeman. "That's the reason. I know what I'm losing if we don't win. A lot of guys don't, not really. Mother, I have to go."

Of course, he went; and of course, Bert and Betty were proud of him. His education, they told each other, could wait until he came back. He was young and there was plenty of time. In the meantime Carolyn would enter college in the fall as had been planned, in spite of the fact that she herself was all for going to South Portland or Brunswick and getting a job in the shipyards. "It won't be any fun in college without Free," she said. "Mother, you've no idea the murder we get away with, with our twin act. And anyhow, have you heard what they pay down there? Even to dopes like me? Why, I could come back simply awash with mink and pearls, and lift the mortgage from the old homestead." Carolyn read omnivorously.

Her father looked at her. "There has never been and never will be a mortgage on this place. I don't like to hear you talk that way, even joking. If you're so set on working, there'll be plenty to do around here this summer, with Free gone. In the fall, you'll go to college, like we always said."

She missed her brother dreadfully that summer. She never once saw Mr. Higgins, although Tim Bartlett reported that he was still alive and well. Tim was what Bert termed "around under foot," and he had the patient nature necessary for a viewing of the ancient trout. Betty was frankly glad of Tim now. He kept Carolyn entertained and helped fill the gap made in her life by her brother's departure. He took her to dances and the movies or just plain riding in his old Chevvy. Both of them had to work during the day, Carolyn helping her mother with the house or the hens, or hoeing the corn or the beans—tasks which would naturally have fallen to Freeman, but which were not too hard for a country girl; and Tim had his own farm to run, another little half-starved ancestral piece hardly worth the bother, except that this year was a good potato year and the Government was paying all-out prices for potatoes to be made into medical alcohol. Tim's father had suffered a stroke in the early spring, so Tim was left with the care of the farm and his father, his mother being long dead. The only time Betty ever heard him complain of his lot, which was not too happy a one for a twenty-year-old, was the day the draft board turned him down. "Agricultural Deferment," he said bitterly. "So I hoe those damn potatoes while Free takes a pop at the bastards. Excuse me, Mrs. Crew."

"That's all right, Tim," Betty said serenely. "I don't like

rough language, but this time I guess you're justified. You're a nice boy."

On the twenty-seventh of August of that year, at ten o'clock in the evening, she had occasion to change her opinion. She was sitting in the kitchen with the Lewiston *Sun* spread out before her on the red-checked tablecloth, looking over the headlines. She and Carolyn had been canning raspberries all day, and she was tired. Carolyn had gone out with Tim; but Bert had stepped on a hay-rake, and half the evening had been spent in soaking and dressing his foot. So this was the first time in over sixteen hours that she had had time to call her soul her own, and she was enjoying it. Bert was asleep, and Carolyn wouldn't be in for an hour or so; but she was all right, because she was with Tim. Betty thought that maybe in a minute she'd get herself a nice cold glass of buttermilk out of the springhouse, to drink slowly as she read the local items, and then before Carolyn came in, she'd take a bath and go to bed. The prospect seemed good to her.

She heard the screen door creak and turned quickly. You never knew when tramps might be around. But it was only Carolyn, with her soft, white, impracticable coat over her arm, and her young face more drawn and pale than Betty had ever seen it. She looked ill and almost old.

"Mother," she said, "I have to speak to you. Tim and I have decided to get married, right away."

This is too much, Betty thought. I'm too tired. But when she spoke, her voice was even. "Let's not talk about it now, dear. You know as well as I do that what you're saying is out of the question. After you're through college, if you still feel the same way about Tim, perhaps— Let's both have a drink of buttermilk and a piece of cake and go to bed." She smiled, but Carolyn, always so responsive, didn't answer her smile.

"A piece of cake," she said despairingly. "Mother, you don't understand. I—I've *got* to marry Tim. I'm going to have a baby."

Betty closed her eyes. In a minute she knew that she wasn't going to die, much as she willed to, so she drew a deep breath and opened them again. Carolyn was still leaning against the door, the planes of her face flat and marble white in the lamplight, her eyes dry and bright. She said thinly, "Mother! Don't look at me like that."

"And how do you expect me to look at you?" Betty didn't recognize her own voice. "I—I just can't understand. This will kill your father, Carolyn. He's set such store by you and Free, and we've done our best for you children, and now you thank us by acting like any common little—"

Carolyn's chin came up. "Don't you say that. It wasn't like that at all. It was— Oh, what's the use? Mother, I am truly sorry about hurting you and Daddy. But I'm not sorry about anything else, and"—her voice rose dangerously—"and don't you try to make me sorry. Don't you blame Tim for this, either. He already feels awful enough about it."

"Then why isn't he in here with you where he belongs, instead of making you face the music alone?"

"He wanted to come in, but I wouldn't let him. I knew how it would be, and— Oh, Mother, do we have to talk like this to each other?" At last the difficult tears streamed down her face, but she still held herself erect. The little Carolyn who had so often flung herself weeping into her mother's arms, sick and sorry to have made her mother sad, was gone forever now; and in her own heartsickness and sorrow, Betty looked at the new Carolyn and saw only defiance and the shameful death of all her dreams.

"It must have been a terrible time for Betty," I said to Catherine at this point. "What did they do? Send Carolyn away to have her baby or—?"

"I'll give the kid credit," Catherine told me. "Probably she could have gone away, but she didn't. She married Tim and stayed right there in town and faced all the talk that always follows a seven months' baby. Gee, you know, Louise, it must have been plain hell for her. She was used to having a good time for herself, running around with the other kids and sort of being queen bee, and all of a sudden here she was, disgraced and saddled with the care of a baby and an old helpless man, besides the housework and, all. And while she wasn't really on the outs with her own family—Betty wouldn't let it be said that she turned her back on her own daughter—still and all, Betty didn't exactly wear her shoes out running over to Carolyn's house."

"But couldn't Carolyn and Tim have moved to another town, or at least couldn't Tim have got a job in the shipyards for a year or two, until it all blew over? Seems to me she was leading with her chin, staying there."

"No." Catherine was definite about it. "In the first place, you forget he was frozen—what an expression!—on the farm by the Government on account of his darned old potatoes. And in the second place, he's like Bert, hipped on the subject of the family homestead. No, she had to stay there if she was to be with Tim. And she was. She's crazy about him."

"Is he crazy about her?"

"He thinks the sun rises and sets in her, which is all right, too; only it didn't make things any easier for her when it

came to getting the wash out and cleaning up Tim's father—
she had to change and wash his bedding sometimes two or
three times a day, and that's no joke—and being snubbed by
the Ladies' Aid. Tim did all he could to help her, but after
all, he had his own work cut out for him. I saw her down to
the store for a minute last time I was over to the Corners, and,
my Lord, what a change! She used to be sort of bubbly and
full of life, but now you'd never know her. She isn't twenty
yet, but she seemed so sort of settled. Her hands looked old.
She had the baby with her, and I will say she keeps him nice.
While I was there, some of the bunch she used to train with
came in, and they stood around drinking pop and joking and
arguing about whether to go to a dance up-country that night,
or to the movies in Farmington. Honestly, Louise, I could
have cried for Carolyn. Not much more than a year before,
she'd been the ring-leader, and they'd all been listening to her,
and in the end, doing what she wanted to do. Now she might
just as well not have been there at all. She just stood off to
one side and listened. I don't blame the other kids. They all
spoke to her friendly enough when they came in. But then
they forgot her, as why shouldn't they? She didn't have anything in common with them any more, but still it was—"
Catherine fumbled for the word and produced rather uncer-
tainly "—sad. The ones I'm really sorry for, though, are Bert
and Betty. It's been terrible for them both, even if they do
take it in different ways."

Bert, that quiet and patient man, took it the way an ox takes
a blow with a sledge hammer, wielded by one whom he has
trusted, between the eyes. He was numbed and staggered and
bewildered, but he went on because nowhere in his philoso-
phy was included the clause that a man was permitted to give

up while yet there remained one deep spring of vitality un-drained. He never went to the store any more. Infrequent late-passers on the road reported seeing his lantern, a steady golden point against the lofty black of the hills, as he sat in the open shed, cutting seed potatoes in the chill of an early spring midnight. He attacked the stony High Pasture, which had always been considered impossible for anything but graz-ing, prying out the rocks which for decades had increased in number as they worked to the surface under the action of heaving frost and eroding weather, worrying them with a crowbar until they were free. Then he would throw the bar down, and before the sweet high clang of iron on stone had died, he was assaulting the insensible masses of granite with his bare hands, performing prodigious feats of brute strength as he bullied them onto the stone-drag. Even then he could not rest, but, wiping the sweat from his haggard face, spoke hoarsely to Belle, the old nag, urging her to where the wall, which was to serve the double purpose of disposing of the stones and fencing the field, grew daily. He seemed a man driven by the Furies as he rolled the stones off the drag and fitted them into their appointed places.

Yet Betty, watching from the kitchen window, sometimes saw him stand, a gaunt silhouette against the skyline, motion-less for long periods, a small filling-rock held forgotten in his hand as he gazed away across the valley toward the hidden house that Carolyn now called home.

And once Nate Pease, hunting a strayed cow up in the Crew woodlot, came out from under the canopy of tender green and glowing red birch and maple buds, across the faded carpet of last year's down leaves, onto the tough, short, blu-ette-sprinkled turf of the High Pasture, and found Bert there, engaged in Herculean struggle with a boulder twice his weight. As any man would, he lent a hand, throwing his bulk where it would do the most good, until the stubborn rock rested firmly on the drag. Then he squatted for a breather on his heels, balancing easily, forearms on thighs, hands hanging limp between his knees, and spoke for the first time as he surveyed the pitted acreage. "Quite a job you done here. What you plannin' to put her into?"

He told about it later, down at the store. "Bert just looked at me like he didn't rightly understand what I meant, or didn't know the answer. 'Course, that's foolish. No man goes to all that trouble to clean up a field, lessen he's got some idee in mind what he's goin' to do with it. Finally I said, 'If 'twas mine, I'd put her into rye the first year, and plow her under, come fall. Then next year, I'd put her into a cash-crop.' He looked at me and looked at the pasture, and then he nodded his head. 'That's what I'll do,' he said. 'Twas as if he hadn't thought to ask himself till right that minute what he was cleanin' up that pasture for. But that don't make sense."

Of course it didn't make sense to Nate. Like all farmers, and especially New England farmers, he had more work ahead of him constantly than he could see his way clear to doing. The undertaking of a gruelling unnecessary task, purely as a therapy for despair, was beyond his understanding.

Betty fought. With head high and lips tight, she attended every meeting of the Ladies' Aid and the Sewing Circle, showing only by the heightened flush on her cheekbones that she noticed the sudden cessation of conversation and the not-quite-quick-enough seizing of a safe topic like the weather that attended her entrance. She knew exactly what "they" had been talking about. They had been talking about Carolyn, and while for decency's sake a show of regret that such a thing should have happened to so nice a girl might have been maintained, and sympathy for Betty might have been punctiliously protested, she knew that underneath these conventional attitudes lay a deep and malicious satisfaction that what had so long been prophesied had come true. They were glad that all the work and planning and purpose of Betty's life had come to naught. She hated them as she sat there, smiling and chatting Spartanly; and sometimes as she went home, head still high and weary shoulders still square, she hated Carolyn.

She shouldn't have to go through this, to have to pretend that everything was fine, that she and Bert were pleased that Carolyn was married to a good boy like Tim Bartlett, that the whole thing had been done with their knowledge and approval, and that, because Carolyn fell on the cellar stairs, the baby had really arrived two months early. Who ever heard of a seven months' baby with hair and fingernails complete? An expression of Freeman's came to her mind: "Who do they think they're fooling?" Who indeed did she think she was fooling? Nobody; nobody at all; but she had to keep on trying, even though sometimes as she lay sleepless in the small hours she recognized with that peculiar light-headed clarity that comes to an exhausted mind and body that it would be better if she simply admitted to the facts. Then perhaps— then almost certainly—the chase ended, the moral victory theirs, the hounds of Virtue would bay on another trail. The talk would stop and people would begin to forget.

Then something happened that made all the fuss and worry about Carolyn's predicament seem trivial. Betty was listlessly washing her breakfast dishes when the radio program to which she was half-listening was interrupted. The announcer,

excitement shaking the careful control of his usual professional tones, announced the attacking of the beaches of Nor-
mandy by Allied task forces. Betty froze, dishmop suspended,
eyes wide, breath held. That meant Freeman. Nobody had to
tell her. She knew. After a minute she put the mop down,
took off her apron—she couldn't have said why—hung it carefully on the hook by the sink, and walked out the door and
up the hill to where Bert was harrowing the High Pasture.

He saw her coming, and waited for her at the end of the
furrow. After she had given him the news, he stood looking
for a long moment out over the countryside spread below this
high field. It was a beautiful day; oh, what a beautiful June
day it was, warm for Maine, and still and golden. The hills
around the valley were softened in a slight haze, and their
gentle, flowing contours melted into each other with an almost poetic rhythm, leading the eye easily up and up to the
faint far mountains of the West. The bark of a dog drifted
clearly up from the valley, and the sound of a hammer pounding briskly. The empty milk-blue sky bent softly over all.
Bert sighed deeply and put his hand on Betty's shoulder in an
unaccustomed gesture of tenderness. "Try not to fret," he
said. "I know it's hard, but—" He broke off, at a loss, and
gazed around again at the lovely, smiling world. "An awful
lot of good boys are dying to-day for this," he said heavily.
"I dunno. Maybe they could do worse." It was a strange sort
of comfort; but somehow Betty was comforted.

It was odd how many people had excuses that day to drop
in at the Crew farm. Nobody had very much to say. One or
two blurted awkwardly that they sure hoped Free was makin'
it all right. That was all; but somehow through the casual
laconic talk of crops and weather and recipes and canning it

was borne in upon Betty that the tide had turned, that this sympathy that was being offered wordlessly had the unmistakable ring of authenticity.

When Freeman came home that fall—for he did come home, with a decoration for valor which he tried to conceal and a slight limp which he could not—he found to his intense dismay that he was a hero. He was the first boy from town to come back, and Jones Corners went all-out to welcome him. Catherine told me about it.

"I guess folks were a little ashamed of themselves for the way they had acted about Carolyn and thought that this was a good chance to sort of make it up to Bert and Betty. I heard a lot of talk about how nice it was that Freeman had turned out so well to kind of balance up for the disappointment his sister had been. They were inclined to be willing to let bygones be bygones. Everybody in town that had a car that would run trimmed it all up with bunting and signs about 'Welcome to Our Hero' and drove over to Livermore to meet the train. The Corners is off the railroad. The band went in one car—it's only five pieces but it doesn't sound too bad outdoors—and all the school kids went in the school bus. They had flags and paper hats and a song to sing that the teacher wrote to the tune of 'Hail the Conquering Hero Comes.' The rest of the cars were packed with everybody in town and his dog, all done up in their best clothes. Freeman, poor kid—I never saw anyone so flusterated. He had to stand there with his ears turning purple and take it, the works—song, speech by the first selectman, cheers, being kissed, by all the girls— heck, I kissed him myself; no wonder he was embarrassed. On top of that, the train crew wasn't going to miss anything, so they held the train till it was over, half an hour at least, with the passengers hanging out the windows. Finally they piled him into the first car with the selectman and his parents and drove back—"

"Wait a minute," I said. "Where was Carolyn all this time?"

"Oh, she was around. Came in a car with Tim and some of his cousins. There wasn't room for her in the car with Freeman." She slanted her handsome eyes at me. "I said folks forgave, but I guess they didn't forget. Or maybe there really wasn't room. I don't know. Anyhow, back at the Corners they gave a banquet in the church basement for Freeman, with more speeches and presentation of gifts, and Lord knows what-all; and everything was peaches and cream. Freeman's getting a medical discharge and he's going on with his education. Of course it won't be the same really as he'd planned. Carolyn won't be with him. Those kids were so close, and they had such a wonderful time together, and of course now that's all over." She examined a fingernail moodily and then burst out, "That's what I hate about war. It spoils everything. None of this would have happened if Freeman hadn't had to go. I know it wouldn't have. It's not only the combat zones that take a pounding. Look at the Crew family. The one thing they did have that amounted to anything was the way they felt about each other. Now it's gone and they haven't anything to put in its place."

Probably she was right, I thought. What was there that could take the place of the kind of natural and spontaneous affection and enjoyment that bound the Crews together? I couldn't find the answer to that one. As it turned out, I didn't have to, because Bert and Betty found it for me. I suppose they spent many evenings seated together in the lamplight by the red-clothed kitchen table, writing and crossing out and rewriting, as they sought the exact and proper wording for the little item that appeared in the Paid Notice column of the *County Journal*, a weekly paper to which Catherine subscribed. She read it aloud to me one evening after supper.

"Mr. and Mrs. Herbert Crew of Jones Corners wish to thank all those who helped to make the welcome home of their son Freeman a success, and they wish to announce that they are also very proud of his twin sister, Carolyn Crew Bartlett of Jones Corners."

I shouldn't have worried. I should have remembered that the Crews, like all the rugged stock from which they sprang, were like the land they lived on. Close under the thin, flower-frothing top-soil that covers the New England hills lies bedrock, which will be neither moved nor altered by any storm that rages over the countryside. All was well with the Crews. They'd got down to the bedrock of character.

5

The Clerks at Spike and Pondy

DURING THE FIRST ten years of my life in this wild and lovely country which I call home, our winter activities were carried on against the background of the lumbering industry. There was never a time when there wasn't a logging camp within walking distance of us, and we were accustomed to the sound of axes ringing through the woods and of trees crashing, back on the ridge. Every morning we were awakened at daylight by the crews going past our bedroom windows to the cuttings, to the jangle and creak of harness, to the voices of men speaking in French or Finnish or the flat Yankee of the locality, to a snatch of song or a fragment of whistled tune. It was a pleasant way to wake up, and I have missed it since this region has been logged off and the camps have moved elsewhere.

The season when I knew Russell Reed and Elmer Rhodes started out as all lumbering seasons start, with the construction crews coming In early in the fall to build the new camps, one a quarter of a mile above us and the other two miles below us, on road and river. A lumber camp consists of at least six buildings. The largest is the bar-room, which is woods parlance for bunkhouse. Then there is the cookhouse, or kitchen, where meals are prepared and served, with a partitioned-off corner where the cook and his helpers sleep, and an unheated ell, called the dingle, for the cold storage of meat. There are the hovel, or stable, and the blacksmith's shop. The office is just what you would expect, a smaller separate shack where the bookwork is done, only in the woods the office also houses the wangan (the store where candy and tobacco and tools and clothes are sold), and the inevitable punchboard; and the clerk usually sleeps as well as works there. The smallest building, except for certain unmentionable little outhouses, is the bosses' shack, where the straw and walking bosses sleep. As you can see, a lumber camp is quite a self-sufficient colony.

When these two camps were done, they had to be called something, for purposes of identification. The one above us, because it overlooked Pond-in-the-River, was called naturally enough simply Pondy. Woodsmen can't be bothered with the intricacies of a name like Pond-in-the-River. The camp below us was called Spike, a fact that baffled Ralph and me for a while, until Syd Abbott, who drove a bulldozer for the contractor, set us right. It turned out that the little spade-bearded French-Canadian carpenter who bossed the construction was named Lebreque. Syd explained reasonably, "You can't very well call a camp Camp Lebreque, can you? So we just named it Spike." And Spike it has remained to this day, when the camp is torn down and the site grown up to raspberry canes and little fir trees as tall as your head. When you live in the middle of one of the blank spaces on the map, any point of reference is valuable, and it's much easier to say, "I saw a bear track down near Spike" than to go into detail like, "about two miles down the Carry, beyond the foot of that long hill, where the river runs along the road."

In the late fall, when the lakes were still open and the ground still free of snow, although the leaves were all down and every sunrise showed a world white with hoar-frost, the personnel of the camps began to filter in. There were the cooks and their helpers, the cookees, and the bosses and the blacksmiths. There were the teamsters, driving the pairs of great horses, and the feeders, who tended the horses and kept the hovels clean. There were the bar-room men—men too old to go into the woods, or else partly incapacitated by some accident when for a moment they had been careless with an ax or with contemptuous familiarity had taken a six-cord load down a slick pitch without snub-line or bridle-chains, but men who could still split wood for the many camp stoves, and keep the bar-room swept and warm. There were the stampers, young men who walked all day alone through the bleak and frozen woods with their little branding hammers in their mittened hands, going from one pile of corded pulp to another, scattered over a fifteen-square-mile area, swinging the stamping iron interminably, imprinting on the ends of each one of the million pieces of four-foot pulpwood the symbol representing the name of the contractor in charge of this particular operation. There were the scalers, lonely men too, with their Bangor scales, who measured the piled wood and accredited to each man the amount he had cut. There were the daymen, paid by the day at a fixed rate for doing whatever the boss told them to do—swamp out, spread road-hay, or work on the landings. There were the yarding crews, working in groups of three as teams, and the stump-cutters, who were so competent that they could make more money working alone on piece rates, or else so at odds with the world that they would rather work alone with only deer and foxes for company than be annoyed with the modern conveniences of co-operation, conversation, and having to put up with their fellow men. And there were the clerks, the white collar class of the lumber camps, who kept the books, ran the wangan, supervised the punchboard, distributed mail, wrote letters for the illiterate, and issued pay in the form of time slips, which in this country are tender as legal as silver dollars anywhere you go.

The first time Ralph and I ever saw Elmer Rhodes, the clerk at Pondy, he was standing in the road in front of the office shack with a little sheaf of letters in his hand, evidently having been warned of our approach by the ungodly clattering of our ancient Model T as it careened over the rutted, stony road. He was in his shirt sleeves, shivering a little in the edged wind that came off the pond to stir his thin gray hair. He looked old and frail and small, alone there against the somber backdrop of woods and mountain and slate-gray open water, as we drew up beside him.

"You're the Riches, aren't you?" he asked. "I'm Rhodes. Wonder if you'd mail these letters for me? Thought I'd get up to Middle myself this afternoon, but the work's piled up on me. You know how 'tis in the fall. The men don't settle down till after the first big snow. Keep shifting from camp to camp, trying to find—I don't know what. One lumber camp's about the same as another, and none of them's perfect. I'd ought to know. Been clerking in them the biggest part of my life. Went into the woods before I was twenty and been in them ever since. You'd think I ought to know my job backwards; used to think so myself. But things ain't like they was in the old days. Comes of the Gov'ment dipping in where it don't belong. All this Social Security." He shook his head. "Complicates the books, and on top of that, half these jokers never heard of the thing. When I make out their time slips, taking out the Gov'ment money, they figure I'm giving them a short scale and put up an argument. Takes up my time trying to explain to the chowderheads. And I ain't as young as I was, nor as patient, for all you'd cal'late I'd be, having reared seventeen children of my own, not to mention a flock of grandchildren—"

I found my voice, which had been startled out of me, temporarily. "Seventeen children!" I exclaimed. "Not *really*, Mr. Rhodes! Or do you mean they seem like seventeen?"

"Nope, there's seventeen of them—or was at last count." He looked both proud and embarrassed. "Keeps my wife busy, now I can tell you, specially since a couple of the married daughters have come home with their young-ones while the husbands are in the Service. Course, they're not all home now, not more'n ten or a dozen—" His voice trailed off. "They go through a lot of shoe leather." He dismissed the subject. "Keeps me hopping, all right. On top of everything else, they've hired a green clerk down below. Never been north of Boston in his life, a city kid fresh out of High School, and I'm obliged to show him the ropes. Reed his name is. Brash little joker. Oh, well." He sighed and handed me the letters. "No sense keeping you here and catching my own never-getover while I tell you my troubles. If you'd just mail these, and if there's anything for us, bring it down?"

We assured him that we certainly would do that; and after that day, until the snow became so deep that we had to put up the Ford and carry the twice-weekly mail and groceries down the two miles of road on our backs, we often did Elmer's errands for him.

I became familiar with the voice of the brash little joker from Boston quite a while before we ever met him, and probably I'd better explain the local custom that made that almost inevitable. I realize that I risk censure in so doing; but here goes, anyhow.

First, it is necessary to make you understand what happens to this country after Labor Day. All summer long it is as though we were giving a large house party, with the entire lake region our house, and much of the civilized world our guests. For three months there is a worldliness and bustle about the countryside. The cars parked at South Arm, the jumping-off point into the wilderness, are Cadillacs and cream-colored Chrysler convertibles with red leather cushions, bearing number plates from New York and Florida and Ontario. The people who knock at your door to ask for a drink of water, or beside whom you fish the river in the freshness of the morning, wear beautiful sports clothes and talk to you beautifully of books and politics and travel, using words which we never use here: words like "predicating" and "casuistry" and "hegira." The mail comes In every single day except Sunday, and when Alys Parsons up-ends the bulging canvas sack onto the counter in the hotel office, preliminary to sorting the day's take, copies of *Kiplinger's Letter* and of the *Herald Tribune* spill out, along with boxes of candy from Bailey's and little packages from Abercrombie's and especially ordered loaves of Pepperidge Farm bread. The lakes are lively with little boats, and it's never safe to go swimming nude in the river. Everything is very gala.

Then comes Labor Day, and it is as if the party had ended

abruptly and all the guests had gone home, leaving the members of the family alone in the vast empty house. Now the mail comes In only twice a week, and the mail sack is a sad, limp affair, with three envelopes and a small package cowering in one corner. The letters are a note to Al from her mother and two bills, and the package is the torn moccasin I sent Out to be stitched. The blue surface of the lake is empty except for Larry's big white boat, slatting to and from the Arm with loads of provisions for the winter. The countryside seems to echo, and for a little while, until we can readjust ourselves to loneliness, we have to reach out for human contacts, to reassure ourselves that we have not been completely deserted. It's the same feeling that prompts the members of the family to draw their chairs up close to the dying fire, after the party is over, for a last chat before going to bed.

That's why we "rubber on the phone," as it is called. It's exactly what it sounds like. When the telephone rings some other number than your own, you carefully remove the receiver from the hook, clamp a muffling hand over the mouthpiece, and listen to whatever conversation may be going over the makeshift line. This I know would be reprehensible in a civilized community, being nothing more nor less than eavesdropping; but it is accepted here, and no one feels guilty about it. You can admit quite shamelessly that you came by any given piece of information "rubbering on the phone." It was by rubbering that I came to know Russell Reed's voice.

It was a fresh young voice—fresh in both senses—lively and gay, a voice incapable of taking anything seriously. Sometimes an excellent mimicry of the Fall-of-Doom manner of Gabriel Heatter would delight my ear. "Oh, there'll be sad hearts in the Home Office this week, yes, tears will flow in the Woods Department. For to-day, as it must to all men, comes to Russell Reed the time when he can't balance his time sheet. Born eighteen years ago in Boston, Reed—"

Elmer was patently less delighted than I. "Cut it out. I'm busy. Bring your books up this afternoon and I'll help you."

"Oh, it's not that serious. Feller came in Wednesday night before supper and signed on, and Thursday after breakfast he decided he didn't like it here. Can you imagine that, Elmer, after all we'd done—? Anyhow, he went Out without paying for the two meals he'd eaten and what am I supposed to do about it?"

"Little late to worry about that," Elmer told him with dry satisfaction. "You should have made him pay, and if he didn't have any money, you should have made him stay till he'd worked it out."

"*Made* him, you say!" Russell's voice rose in horror. "He was twice as big as me. Three times as big. *Made* him! Ha! Well, what do I do now? Just forget him?"

It was Elmer's turn to be horrified. "You can't— He had two meals and someone's got to pay."

"Wouldn't it be simpler—?" Russell began wistfully, and added hastily on Elmer's outraged, indrawn breath: "All right, all right, I'll pay myself; but I still think—"

The first time I ever saw Russell Reed he was on horseback. I was up in the top of the woodshed, getting down the snowshoes that we hang on wires there during the summer, to keep them dry and safe from mice, when I heard a distant drifting cry of "Hi-yo, Silver!" My first reaction was that I'd gone woods queer at last. When you start hearing voices, it's supposed to be bad. But before I had time to worry much, one of the big, shaggy twitch horses from Spike wheeled into the driveway. I knew the rider must be the new clerk. Woodsmen seldom ride the horses, and never wear blue serge suits and unbuckled galoshes. So I pitched the snowshoes down onto the sawdust pile and swung myself down after them.

"Hello," I said. "You must be Reed. What can I do for you?"

"Well, frankly, it wasn't my idea to turn in here. This is the first time I've ever been on horseback, and nobody told me horses have minds of their own. You got any helpful suggestions?"

I laughed. "It's considered easier to do with a saddle, but if you want to learn the hard way, bareback—"

"Nobody's got a saddle. Say, you haven't got a pair of skates I can borrow? I want to go skating before the snow covers the ice. Do you know anything about skiing? I've ordered some skis. I'm going to do a lot of skiing this winter. Maybe I'd better get some snowshoes, too." He looked at the pairs on the sawdust. "Never saw a pair like that. What's the advantage?"

I explained that they were bear-paws, and although I myself didn't like them much, as they always seemed to me to be nose-heavy, they were considered good off the trails, as they had no tails to tangle in the brush.

"I guess I'd better get that kind then. I want to explore this whole country while I'm here. Oh, and look. Have you got any books I could borrow? Time sort of drags in the evening."

I assured him that we had all kinds of books and asked

him if he wanted to come in right then and pick some out.

"Gee, I'd like to, but if I ever get off this beast now, I'll never get on again. Besides, I thought I'd go up to Pondy and heckle Elmer. What a guy! Nothing but work, work, work. What's the percentage in that? What does he want to sit in the office all the time for, adding up columns?"

I thought of poor Elmer, bowed eternally over his books, his pale face forever puckered with worry. "Maybe Elmer wants to hold his job," I said meanly. "Maybe you'd better not make too many plans, because it's just possible that the company didn't hire you to ride horseback and ski and skate and explore."

He laughed. "Don't worry. I get my work done. I got system, see. Trouble with Elmer is he takes things too serious. It drives him nuts to see anyone have a good time."

"Oh, I don't think that's quite fair. He just feels responsible for you and doesn't want you to get fired."

"Don't kid yourself. He's just fussy. I'm trying to teach him to have a flexible mind, like mine."

"You'll have flexible employment if you're not careful," I told him. "Not that it's any of my business."

"Nope," he agreed cheerfully, and clucked to the horse, who seemed to have fallen asleep on its feet. "Can't find the starter on this thing. Give him a bat on the rear, will you, Mrs. Rich?" I delivered the bat, and he went off, hi-yoing at a great rate. He was a cute kid, I thought, even if he was a little too cocky; but he wouldn't last very long on this job.

I was wrong. The deer season ended and the lakes sealed over and the snow piled deeper and deeper in the woods. The sun rose later and later, and, barely skimming the ridges to the south, set earlier and earlier. Christmas passed, and the cold strengthened, striking deeper and deeper toward the heart of heat which means life in the North, whether it is the core of warmth that a man carries about in his own body, or the carefully tended fires of his dwellings. Russell Reed should have, by my reckoning, long since run home, defeated, to the city streets that he knew, to the steam-heated apartment, the easy entertainment of movies and Saturday night dates, to the comfortable, gregarious job as soda jerk in the neighborhood drugstore for which his undeniable good looks and sassy manner so well fitted him. But still he rollicked about the country. His rather weedy frame filled out and he took on an appearance of great physical well-being, probably because of the gigantic lumber camp meals and the many hours he spent in the open. He acquired a suitable wardrobe of heavy pants and buffalo-checked shirts, along with remarkable proficiency on skis and snowshoes, and became in short a good woodsman, although slightly in the Hollywood tradition. So I gave up worrying about him, if ever I did worry, partly because he didn't need my concern, but mostly because along about this time we came to realize the truly desperate circumstances that engulfed Elmer.

I guess we'd been pretty blind. We'd see Elmer a couple of times a week as we went past the Pondy office, bending over his desk, working on his books; but as Russell was now carrying his mail, since we were all on foot, we very seldom had occasion to more than wave at him through the window, or at most drop in to buy cigarettes or candy from the wangan. He seemed about the same as usual—possibly a little thinner and grayer, with a nervous habit of licking his lips and cracking his knuckles—so we didn't think much about him, except that he ought to get out in the fresh air more.

Then one still, bitter night I found myself sitting bolt upright in bed. I could hear Ralph breathing deeply and quietly, and the snap of a timber as it contracted in the cold. The white light of the moon lay in a slim wedge on the counterpane, and the cold flowed in an almost visible current through the window which stood open onto the road, ten feet away. There was nothing that could have awakened me, I thought, as I listened and checked off the familiar, natural sounds. Then I heard the slow, spaced squeaking of footsteps on the frozen snow of the Carry. Something was outside, walking back and forth; a bear, perhaps—and the window was only three feet from the ground. I slid out of bed and tiptoed across the floor, intent on closing the window quietly. I'd seen what a bear can do, once it gets inside a camp, and I wanted to be no part of any such shambles.

But it wasn't a bear outside. It was Elmer, thin and black as the shadow of a dead tamarack in the unearthly cold light of the moon. There was something about him that frightened me, although I can't say now what it was. I was only half awake, and I guess I thought that he was a ghost, silly as that sounds. He must have heard me, because he turned his head in my direction. His face was blue in the moonlight, and his eyes seemed sightless. My mouth was dry, and I was cold to my bones. Then I knew how ridiculous I was being, and I spoke to him. "Hello, Elmer. What's the trouble?"

Behind me Ralph asked, his voice blurred with sleep, "Wassa ma'er?" but Elmer only looked at me out of his hollow eyes.

"Elmer," I said sharply, "I'm freezing to death. Go around to the door and I'll let you in. It's warm in the living room."

"I'll let him in." Ralph was awake now. "Poke up the fire and start some coffee. Maybe he's sick."

The living room *was* warm, and I had everything I needed on hand. There were even some sugar cookies in a tin. I lighted all the lights, and the golden glow of kerosene lamps was soft and warm after the icy moonlight into which I had been staring. Elmer stood inside the door, shivering, with his cap in his hands, his shoulders hunched, his chin down, until Ralph said, "Take off your jacket and sit down. In a minute we'll have some coffee. We haven't seen you to talk to for a coon's age. What's new?"

He raised his head. "I—I think I'm going crazy. I-I can't think. I can't sleep or eat or— Do you think I'm going crazy?" His eyes blazed directly at me, and I thought: I have Ralph, and in an emergency a good stout piece of stove wood to stash his head in.

So I said, "For Heaven's sake! I never heard of anything so foolish. Of course you're not going crazy— Here, sit down and drink this coffee. Sugar? Cream? Have a cookie— Don't you know that when people think they are going crazy, it's a sure sign that they aren't? Everybody says so. But if you're really worried about yourself, why don't you go Out for a week end? Not that you need to, but you haven't seen your family for ages, and the change would do you good."

"Do you really think so?" he asked eagerly. Then his shoulders sagged. "I can't. I can't take the time off. I'm be-hind in my work now, and if I ever lose my job, I don't know what would become of the folks. I have to keep my job, if it kills me."

"You won't be much good to your folks dead," Ralph

stated a little brutally. "Do what Louise says. Take a vacation. Russell can do your work for a few days."

He jumped to his feet, spilling coffee. "I—I don't want him to do my work! It's bad enough to have him rubbing it in all the time that he can do his own easier than I can. I—I won't have him monkeying with my books! You hear me?"

"Oh, take it easy," Ralph said. "He's not a bad kid—just a little young and fresh, that's all. He'd be glad—"

"I won't have it! I'd rather—almost anything—than go meeching around him, asking favors. He makes fun of me all the time—"

"Why, no, he doesn't either," I remonstrated. "Or at least, no more than he does everyone. It's just his idea of a joke, to ride people. Just ignore him."

But Elmer was beyond speech. He stood there trembling. Then he snatched up his cap. "Well, I've got to get back to work," he said dully. "Thanks for the coffee. I feel a little better now. Good-night."

Ralph and I sat up until daybreak, discussing the situation, but the only conclusion that we could come to was that one of us had better speak to Russell, and suggest that he stop pestering Elmer for a while. As Ralph had said, he was a good kid—just a little too young to have much imagination.

As it happened, it wasn't necessary, because Russell brought the matter up himself the next afternoon, when he stopped in to change some books. We heard him talking to the dog as he took his skis off outside, and then stamping the snow off his boots on the porch. He banged once on the door and entered, as is the custom of the country. For once his handsome face was serious, and his greeting restrained. He came at once to the matter that was bothering him.

"You folks seen Elmer lately? What ails him? I think he's going crazy."

"What makes you think that?" I asked cautiously.

"Well, I was just up there, and he was raving and tearing and carrying on. What started it—when I went in he was adding up a column of figures for the third time, and he'd got a different answer every time. All I said was, 'Why don't you do like I do?'—and he never even gave me a chance to finish. He threw his pencil on the floor and started yelling about how everybody was in a plot to make his work harder. He didn't make much sense, but it sounded as though he thought I was responsible for starting Social Security, just to foul him up. Just then the scaler came in, so I got out. Gee, what an excitable guy! Has he always been like that?"

"I don't think so." I told him. "But you see, he has a lot of family responsibility, and he worries. Then of course he's been keeping books one way for over forty years, and he can't get used to a new way. You must remember he's an old man, and it's hard for him to change, and I suppose it hurts his pride to have a new clerk like you do the work so easily, and—"

"Gee, why didn't someone tell me? I'd be glad to help him, only when I first came here, he acted as if he'd invented the books, always telling me what was wrong with mine. I didn't think he'd relish any suggestions from me. Why, I could bring my adding machine up a couple of days a week, and—"

"You could bring what up?" I asked.

"My adding machine. I rented one for the winter, when I found out what I had to do. Why, I'd *never* get done without it. Of course, it won't do all the work for you, but it sure saves a lot of time and mistakes."

I looked at him bitterly. "And I've been giving you credit for being so smart!"

"Well, isn't it smart to do your work the easiest way? But like I was saying— I could lend him— Only now he's so sore at me, probably he wouldn't use it anyhow. He's in a terrible state. If I'd known— You don't suppose my kidding him really bothers him, do you?"

I decided to tell the truth. "Yes, I do; but I think it would help his morale just to know you've been using an adding machine, whether he wants to use it himself or not. He's lost confidence in himself, I guess, and if he could get it back—"

The next day along about sunset Russell knocked on the window. "Can't take time to get my skis off and come in, or I'll be late for supper. Just wanted to tell you Elmer has the adder, and I've showed him how to run it. He's all pepped up about it, and everything's under control."

For a few days it did seem that way. Elmer stopped walking the Carry in the night, and when we waved to him through his window, he seemed almost cheerful. But unfortunately things aren't that easy of solution in real life, no matter how neatly they may work out on paper. The next thing that happened was that Elmer began distrusting the adding machine. It didn't seem sensible to him, so he said, that a gadget could do brainwork; so he checked every total himself, and it wasn't long before he was worse off than ever.

"I try and try to tell him," Russell said to us, "that that machine doesn't make mistakes, but he won't listen. Honest, I'm worried about him. I feel to blame—"

"I don't think you should," I said. And I really didn't.

"After all, most people can take a little riding without going off their base. It isn't your fault. It's just that everything's too much for him."

Russell looked grateful for this reassurance. "I'd certainly hate to think— You know, I must have been an awful little stinker when I came in here. Gee, it seems a long time ago!"

It did to me, too. "You've grown up some," I told him. "What made you come here in the first place?" I'd been wanting to know for a long time.

"I guess I read too many books. I wanted to go some place where there was room and mountains and snow and adventure, and the only jobs I could get in the city were dumb. So I answered an ad in the paper— Well, I got what I wanted all right, and now I'll never be satisfied with anything else, I guess." He brooded. "Well, I've got to get going. I told Elmer I'd stop in this afternoon."

It was only a few days after that that the telephone rang early in the morning. It was the scaler at Pondy. "Elmer down there?"

"No. Why would he be down here at this time of day?"

"Couldn't say. Only he isn't around here, and his bed hasn't been slept in. They haven't seen anything of him at Middle, either. I'll call Spike. Might be he went down there." I stayed on the line while he put his call through and heard Russell say that he hadn't seen Elmer since day before yesterday. "I'll come right up," he added. "Maybe I'll meet him on the road." Shortly after I saw him going by the house fast on his skis, and after what I considered a decent interval, I called Pondy back.

The scaler answered. "Nope, we ain't found him yet, but most of his stuff is gone, including his snowshoes, and Russell says there's fresh snowshoe tracks turning off the road onto the B Pond trail. Any of you been over that way in the past day or two? No? Then it looks like he just packed his switchel and flew. He could make Upton all right, and from there he could catch the stage to Bethel and get home." A muffled colloquy followed, and the scaler came back on again. "Russell's worried for fear he's jumped into the river or something foolish. He's going to follow the tracks and make sure he's okay." He hung up.

Russell was back by mid-afternoon, with his mackinaw swinging open and his cap shoved back on his head, in spite of the freezing weather. "Whew, that's hot work," he said. "I made time. Went clear over to the highway that leads into Upton. I lost his tracks there. There'd been a lot of traffic over the road. Anyhow, I figured that if he got that far, he was all right. It's only a mile into town, and all good road. What I was afraid of was that he'd made up his mind to do away with himself, and I kept expecting to find—But I didn't." He leaned on his ski poles, dug into the snow. "I'm sort of relieved. He needed a vacation, although it was kind of funny, his going off without saying a word. But probably the notion hit him, and he just went. He'll be okay when he gets back." He thrust his poles powerfully, setting himself into motion. "Got to get back to the salt mines. Haven't done a stroke of work to-day, and what with my own books and Elmer's, Mrs. Reed's little boy is going to be busy."

But the days went by and Elmer didn't come back, nor was any word of him received. A couple of letters came In from his wife, the last one mailed long after Elmer should have arrived home; so finally the boss decided reluctantly, because he was loath to interfere with the private life of anyone as harmless as Elmer, that something ought to be done. "I hate to set the state cops on his trail," he said. "He ain't done nothing wrong. Russell says his books and money balance. Only if anything's happened to him, his folks ought to know. Before I call the cops, cal'late I'll go over to Upton and see what they know about him there."

Nobody in Upton had seen hide nor hair of him, and in a town of that size someone would have, if he'd been there at all. It was as if he had been snatched into thin air at the point where his snowshoe tracks ended on the beaten surface of the road. He'd never gone into the village; that was certain. Where, then, had he gone? There was no other town within walking distance, and a canvass of the farms along the highway revealed nothing. It seemed obvious that he had been given a lift by a passing car, and in that case it was a problem for the police. Woodsmen had, before then, been picked up and robbed and murdered for their few belongings, and their bodies dumped off in the woods or thrust under the ice of lake or river. So for a short while there was a feverish search for Elmer, with the usual futile excursions and false alarums; but it all came to exactly nothing. After a while the excitement died down, there was a new clerk at Pondy, and we didn't even talk about Elmer very often, except, when conversation lagged, to speculate idly on what did actually happen to him.

Late in March the camps closed and the crews went Out. Russell Reed, one of the last to leave, came in one morning to tell us good-bye. "We'll miss you," I told him sincerely. "I suppose you're going home to Boston?"

"Sooner or later. I thought I'd sort of look the rest of this country over a little, as long as I'm up this way. I thought I'd go over into New Hampshire and Vermont, and maybe do a little real skiing. Some of the winter sports places are still open. I'll let you know how I'm getting on; and if you happen to hear anything about Elmer, will you let me know? I've kind of got him on my mind still."

I didn't realize until much later just how much on Russell's mind Elmer really was; so much, in fact, that the proposed skiing trip was merely a blind for what actually amounted to a personal, one-man search for him. I met Russell quite by accident one day, after the ice had gone out, on Congress Street in Rumford, where I'd gone to shop for the first time in eight months. After we'd greeted each other and he'd informed me that he'd never before seen me in a skirt and I looked funny, we decided that he had time for a quick cup of coffee before he had to catch the afternoon train down-country. We have two trains a day, and the first one leaves too early in the morning for most people.

"Where've you been and how've you been and all about it?" I said after we were seated. "Don't ask me about things up on the lakes, because everything is the same as usual, and everybody's fine, and—I know you're going to ask—nothing has ever been heard from Elmer."

He stirred his coffee thoughtfully, his head bent. Then he looked at me. "Mrs. Rich, how good are you at keeping your mouth shut?"

"I'm not sure." I told him truthfully. "Pretty good, I guess, if it's important that I should."

"Well, this is important." He looked around in a conspiratorial manner and lowered his voice. "I found Elmer. Shhh!" he admonished hastily as I started to exclaim. He really was an awful kid still, I thought; all this elaborate hush-hush business. "You see," he went on, "I knew he couldn't have much money with him, so I figured that if he was still alive, he'd have to get a job somewhere. He'd have to go far enough away so he wouldn't run much risk of meeting someone who knew him, but he couldn't go too far, because he didn't have the price. I figured that he'd try for a lumber-camp clerking job, since that was all he knew how to do, and he'd probably pick some small job, run by an independent operator, because that way he'd run less chance of being recognized by the regular woodsmen who float around from company camp to company camp. Then I inquired around where there might be a set-up like that. New Hampshire was too near, so I decided to take a look around northern Vermont and York State. Part of the time I made out like I was looking for work myself, and part of the time I pretended I was just a skiing nut. I didn't take anyone's word for anything, because I figured maybe he'd be using another name, and whatever it was wouldn't mean anything to me. I had to see for myself. And sure enough, I found him over in Vermont in a little camp back in the hills."

He looked to me for approval, so I said, meaning every word of it, "I think you're wonderful, Russell! Tell me, how does he look, and how *is* he, *really?*"

"He looks swell. He's grown a beard and put on some weight, and he says he likes his job. He's only got twenty-five men, and he can handle that easy enough. I'm not going to tell you the name he's going by, or where he is. Not that I don't trust you," he added politely, "only the fewer people that know a secret, the better, I think. Don't you?"

I said that I certainly did. "But why does it have to be

a secret? If he's all right now, I think his family ought to know—"

"*No!* If you could have seen the look on his face when I walked in—like a wild animal in a cage! I thought he was going to jump through the window. *No.* Don't you see? He feels free now, for the first time since he was twenty, and if he has to go back to the cage—"

"Now really, Russell," I said tartly. "Aren't you being a little melodramatic? And remember, it's a cage—if you must call it that—that he made himself. What about his poor wife, worrying about him, and for all you know, starving to death? At least she ought to be told that he's alive and well, even if you don't want to go into details. I don't think it's fair—"

"She's got millions of grown-up kids to take care of her. She won't starve. And if they know he's alive, they'll find him. They'll mean well, but— If I'd thought you were going to be like this, I'd never have told you. Give the poor devil a break, Mrs. Rich. I *tell* you that if they catch up with him and make him go back now, he'll go stark, staring mad!" He shook his head impatiently and started again. "Look, give him time. Maybe after a while he'll go back of his own accord; and even if he doesn't, isn't it better to have his family worry a little—they'll get over it; they're probably through the worst of it already—than to have him shut up in Augusta the rest of his life? Then they really would have something to worry about."

"Well," I said slowly, "I don't know." I looked at him. All the things that I had thought made him such an attractive kid were completely wiped out of his face—the impudence, the insouciance, the gay recklessness. He looked a little stern and very serious. And suddenly I wondered why I was in such a dither. Why, it wasn't my problem at all. That fresh brat Russell Reed had made it his, had taken over the full responsibility, and it had made a man of him, a man whose judgment should and could be trusted. There was no excuse at all for me to interfere.

"Okay," I said. "Now if you intend to catch that train—"

All this was quite a while ago, and there isn't very much to add, except that the next Christmas Eve, Elmer walked into his own home unannounced, more hale and hearty and happy than he had been in years. It made quite a stir at the time, and the final official verdict was temporary amnesia. He bought a little store with the money he'd saved during his mysterious absence and has done very well with it. And last Christmas I got a card from Russell Reed. He'd spent the war with the ski-troopers, where the going had been rugged but interesting, I gathered. At the writing, he was in Alaska, which he assured me was much better than Maine. Maine was all right, of course, for kids such as he'd been, and for old ladies. He didn't say "like you," but I suspect that's what he meant. Yes, Maine was all right; but Alaska, now, was real country.

6

And She Be Fair

WHEN THE TELEPHONE rang on that gray November morning, I was just finishing up the last of the breakfast dishes. I tossed the wiper over the line near the stove with one hand, took down the receiver with the other, and said, "Hello, Joe" into the ugly, battery-powered, and completely indispensable wall set. There are five families strung out along the fifteen miles of single, uninsulated wire that loops and sags through the woods from the Parsonses' at Middle Dam to the Brown Farm in Magalloway Plantation, and after you've lived with the rather makeshift contraption for a while, you get so you can identify each individual on the line by his ring. Sure enough, Joe Mooney's beautiful, deep voice —which was all I knew of him, since I had never seen him— drifted easily over the miles of swamp and mountain that separated us to mingle in my kitchen with the singing of the tea-kettle, the crackling of the fire in the range, and the whine of the dog wanting-in at the door.

"Louise," he said, "have you people seen anything of a young couple over your way? They went into the woods ten days ago, and they were supposed to be back at the end of the week. They haven't showed up, and their folks are getting worried."

That was easy to answer. We hadn't seen a strange face or heard a strange voice for over a month. "But they might be up at Middle," I added. "What are they doing anyhow, hunting?"

"I've already called the Parsonses and Millers and they're not around there. Yeah, they're hunting. They're on their honeymoon. Struck off up-country right after the ceremony. The fellow's on leave from the Army, and he's going to be AWOL in another ten minutes, more or less, if he isn't already. Their car's still where they left it, parked in True Durkee's field in Upton, so— Look, Louise, is Ralph doing anything special this morning? Maybe he'd drive down to Sunday Cove and take a look around? You see, they set off in a boat up Umbagog—"

"Sure," I promised. Joe's asking was the emptiest formality. When anybody gets lost in this country, everybody drops everything to look for them. We all realize more fully than any town-dweller possibly can that man is pretty insignificant when pitted against the forces of Nature, and that knowledge binds us into a mutually protective fraternity. We know that in spite of our best efforts and precautions, the time may well come when any one of us will be lying on the back of a desolate ridge with a broken ankle and night drawing in, and then the only thing that will stand between us and pure panic will be the certainty that if we just sit tight, someone will come and get us out. So I said, "Sure. I'll let you know when we get back, Joe."

Looking for people lost in a hundred square miles of woods isn't quite the hopeless task that it sounds. Actually there are only a few places where they are likely to be. This young man and his bride should be easier than most to find, equipped as they were with a boat, which they would have to draw up somewhere along the lake, and all of the paraphernalia for a week's camping, which they certainly weren't going to carry about on their backs all day. They'd have to leave it at one of the few possible camp sites, which they would undoubtedly use as a base. So Ralph and I didn't bother much about beating the bush and hallooing on the three-mile trip to Sunday Cove. We made one side excursion to Smooth Ledge, because that is a lovely place to camp, but there was nothing there except the green water pouring smoothly over the ledges, a cold fireplace with the ashes still soggy from the rain of ten days before, and a partridge sitting in a stunted cedar.

As we coasted down the last long rough hill to the cove, we heard the sound of an outboard, throttled low, and I felt a lift of the spirit. Everything was all right. These people, whoever they were, were safe. They'd just lost track of the time, an easy thing to do in the woods, especially if you're on your honeymoon. Each day flows smoothly into the next, with nothing to distinguish one from the other except a change in the weather or some outstanding event, like the shooting of a deer or the blooming of the first dandelion. But when we came out of the woods and drew up beside the caved-in remains of an old lumber camp, we saw Cliff Wiggin-Wallace hunched in the stern of his battered old boat, slowly circling the glassy waters of the cove. We gave him a hail, and he came in to where we were standing on the steeply shelving ledge that serves as a landing.

"Mornin'," he said, cutting his motor. "What you folks

doin' down here so early?" We told him and he nodded. "Me, too. Joe give me a ring a while ago. I've been over every inch of shoreline 'twixt here and my place, and I ain't seen hide nor hair of a livin' soul. I figure now on goin' over and followin' the New Hampshire side down. Might be they're over there." He squinted at the sky from under the brim of his disreputable old hat. "She's brewin' up some weather. Don't like the looks of it. Come to-morrow, we'll have snow." He changed the subject abruptly. "You ain't got a piece of two-inch angle-iron up to your place, Ralph? I'm fixin' up my saw rig—"

They were off. Where in towns people meet and chat on corners, or in the drugstore or post office, we carry on our casual social contacts on lonely shores or boat landings, or along trails leading to nowhere of importance, or occasionally in the middle of lakes, shouting from boat to boat. When Cliff and Ralph began to show signs of staying there the rest of the morning arguing about V-belts, I whistled to the dog, off on some private errand, to create a diversion. Cliff knew Kyak was a boat-riding fool, and that if once he got aboard it would take more than the three of us to get him back ashore; so he started winding the cord of his outboard.

"I'll be gettin' along," he said. "You might let Joe know where I'm at; save me the trouble of callin' him." He yanked on the cord, the motor roared into life, and he lifted a limp hand in farewell and headed out of the cove toward New Hampshire.

To tell the truth, I didn't think much more about the lost young couple that day, after I'd called Joe up and given him my report. I was busy with the housework and all the tasks outdoors and in that have to be done in November, in preparation for the long winter ahead. If I had any attitude about the whole affair, it was that everything possible was being done to find them, backed by a sort of subconscious confidence that they'd turn up safe and sound eventually. I'd lived through dozens of excursions and alarums centering about lost hunters during my ten years of life in the backwoods. Sooner or later they always showed up none the worse for wear, and my sweat, blood, and tears were so much wasted energy. But along about sunset there was a knock on the kitchen door, and I opened it to find Fred Judkin, from Upton, standing on the step with an older man, a stranger, at his shoulder.

I hadn't seen Fred since before he went into the Army, so I greeted him with great enthusiasm, telling him how nice he looked in uniform—which probably disgusted him—and asking him if they'd got their deer. I assumed he was home on leave and was improving his time by hunting. But when he stepped into the mellow light of the kitchen, I saw that he wasn't carrying a gun and that his face was tired and serious. He introduced his companion as Mr. Kennicott, and they both sank down wearily into chairs by the stove, with the air of men who had a long hard day behind them. "Ralph will be right in," I said, "and then we'll have supper. You'll sleep here, of course? You can't start back to Upton at this time of day. It'll be pitch-black in half an hour."

"That's what I was wondering, Louise—if we could stay the night here. When we started out, we planned on getting home to-night, but it's taken us longer than we thought, and anyhow—" He nodded significantly at Mr. Kennicott, who was sitting with his head bowed and his eyes closed in one of the straight, uncomfortable kitchen chairs. His face was gray with fatigue and his lips looked pinched. So far he had made no comment beyond a courteous greeting, but now he remarked a little apologetically, "I'm not as young as I was. It's taken it out of me, the walking and the worrying, but I had to come—"

"It's Mr. Kennicott's boy that's lost," Fred broke in quietly. "He's in my outfit. I know this country, so the Army gave me emergency leave—"

The door opened, and Ralph and Kyak came in on a wave of cold air. I explained our guests to him, and he said, "Wow! You mean you've followed the shore of Umbagog all the way up to here? It must be twenty miles."

"Not quite," Fred told him. "A couple of other parties started out to search the shore nearer Upton, so we took the old Magalloway Trail as far as the town line, and cut down to the lake from there. Even so, it was tough enough. I was counting on Cliff to set us across the river, but he wasn't home. We had to walk up the other side as far as the dam, before we could get across. You been over there lately? Nothing but blowdown and swamp holes."

"It's been that way ever since the hurricane," Ralph told him. "You must be half starved. When do we eat, Louise?"

I hastily put two more plates and a handful of silver onto the table. "Right now. Ralph, see who wants coffee and who wants tea, and I'll call Cliff and Joe up to hear if there's any news." But Joe didn't answer the two long rings that were his signal, and I remembered then that he closed the switchboard at six and went home, at that time of the year. So I rang four times for Cliff. After a minute he said, "Hello."

"Any news of those people who are lost?" I asked, and he said that there wasn't.

"Went down the New Hampshire side as far as Moll's Rock, and all in through Leonard's Pond, and I didn't see a trace of no one. So I come along home. I figure no news is good news." I said yes, that's what I figured, too, and hung up.

After supper, rested and relaxed by the hot meal, we moved into the living room and drew chairs up around the open fire. The wind had started to whine down-river, whuffling around the corners of the house like a coursing hound. I went from window to window, pulling the faded red draperies together with a muted clash of rings on rods, to shut out the night. At the last one I stood for a moment in the shadow beyond the circle of firelight and looked at the room. Outside in the lonely darkness the wind beat insistently against the glass, and the wild roar of the river swelled and faded on the gusts. Inside it was quiet, except for the rustle of the fire on the hearth and the quiet breathing of the sleeping dog. The three men sat silent, sunk low in their chairs, their long legs stretched out to the blaze and their eyes fixed on the leaping flames. A window rattled behind the drawn curtains and I shivered, although the room was warm.

As though he knew what I was thinking, Mr. Kennicott said in his quiet voice, "I hope they're warm enough to-night."

Ralph spoke quickly. "It isn't really cold out—not much below freezing. It'll be easy to keep comfortable to-night, if they know anything at all about the woods." He made it a question.

"Oh, yes. Yes. All their lives they've been crazy about the woods, both of them. Why, even when they were kids—" his eyes lighted and his tired face came alive—"even when they were kids, they knew the woods better than some guides.

They'd light out as soon as they'd had their breakfasts, and sometimes we wouldn't see them again until sun-down. We've got some pretty rough country down our way—not like this, of course, but wild enough—but we never worried about them. My boy got his first deer when he was twelve." He laughed. "That was a proud day for him. I can see him now, trying to act as if it were nothing, and him not much taller than his gun. Couldn't touch him with a ten-foot pole all that fall. Kind of put Mary's nose out of joint—Mary's his wife now—but she got an eight-point buck two years later. She was thirteen then, a skinny little thing with her hair all every-which-way, running around in work pants and a plaid shirt. You couldn't hardly tell her from another boy. It wasn't till she was sixteen or so that she turned pretty all of a sudden.

"It's a funny thing how some girls do that. She came into the house one morning—she and Jack were planning on going fishing that day—and I looked at her and thought to myself, 'Well, son, it won't be long now. You're going to get used to a little competition pretty soon.' When they get as good-looking as Mary is, they usually lose interest in hunting and fishing and scrambling up mountains and knocking around in boats. It's only natural that they outgrow their tom-boy days. Jack had never shown Mary any special consideration, and I didn't imagine it would occur to him to start now. The first time they ever went fishing—he was seven and she was six—'twas down to the mill-pond. They cut two poles and rigged them up with twine and some old hooks they found 'round the house and dug themselves a canful of worms. Mary baited her own hook, you'd better believe. They caught a mess of little perch, and you'd better believe too that Mary cleaned her own. Don't know but what she cleaned his, too. He was just enough older, and a boy—you know how it is. The way a little girl like that would look at it, he was doing her a favor letting her hang around with him, and she felt she'd ought to pay her way by doing more'n her share of the dirty work. Not that he was mean or hateful to her, ever. He wasn't. It was just that he treated her like a kid brother; and her folks and Ma and me, we were glad it was that way. Made it nice all around, living next door to each other, the way we do." He smiled into the fire. After a minute he went on.

"That's why in a way I was sorry that day she turned pretty. Oh, I don't suppose it was as fast as all that, but it seemed so to me. I'd seen her just the day before, and she'd looked the same as always—little thing with eyes too big for her face and her hair cut short and curly. She kept it short to save bother, but it curled of its own accord. Then the next morning—" he paused, looking a little puzzled— "next morning it was still short and curly. Come to think of it, she even had on the same clothes—blue jeans rolled half-way up to her knees and an old shirt Jack had outgrown, with the sleeves pushed up above her elbows. But out of a clear sky it struck me that there was one awful pretty girl. Maybe it was the way she laughed, with her head thrown back; or maybe it was how she handled herself, quick and business-like, but at the same time as graceful as a swallow. Whatever it was, I thought to myself that the boys would be flocking around her pretty soon, taking her to the movies and buying her sodas. Naturally she'd like it, and who could blame her; but then where would Jack be? He'd think it was silly to offer to carry one little bit of a half-pound book home from school for her, when he knew she could walk all day with a thirty-pound pack on her back.

"Mary's awful deceptive to look at. She's little; looks as though you could break her in two with your bare hands. But she's tough as nails. She can do anything my boy can do, and some things she can do better'n he can. Swim, for instance. Jack's a good swimmer, but Mary—she's a champion. She's as much at home in the water as on dry land. That's one reason I'm not worried as much as I might be about them now. Allowing their boat swamped—though I don't know any reason why it should have, with them brought up around boats and knowing how to handle them—but allowing it did, they'd get ashore as easy as rolling off a log. No, I'm not worried about that."

He fell silent while Ralph hauled himself to his feet and put another birch log on the fire. The sparks flew up the chimney as the loose bark caught, and the room was suddenly flooded with leaping red light. Somewhere a shutter banged dully, and at the window over the river the curtain swayed slightly in the draft around the sash. But the air in the room remained so still that the smoke from our cigarettes rose unwavering toward the raftered ceiling. It was as though we four were in a sheltered pool of quiet, safe from the rushing torrent of the wind passing over us. Then the fire settled down to a slow, steady burning, and Mr. Kennicott went on, almost as though he were talking to himself.

"What I figure has happened, one of them got hurt. It's easy to do in the woods. You slip on a mossy rock and break your leg, or you catch your foot in a crevice and sprain your ankle. I don't figure they had a shooting accident. They both know too much about guns for that. No, one of them is hurt, and the other can't leave to get help. They don't know this country at all. They don't know where people live, or how to get to them. If it were down home now— But it isn't, and all they can do is the sensible thing: wait to be found. They know that as soon as they're over due, we'll be out searching. Just as sure as I'm sitting here, they're holed in somewhere, snug as you please. They've got good warm sleeping bags and plenty of food, and they know how to set up a comfortable camp. I always say, and it's true, that you don't have to worry about two people in the woods. Two people can get out of almost anything. It's when a man's alone that you have to worry."

We all nodded, because what he said was reasonable and had in the past proven true, except in a very few, exceptional cases; and we all thought, although no one said it, that they both must be alive, since in the event of a fatality, the survivor would have made his way to help immediately. I wanted to hear the rest of the story of Jack and Mary, so I asked, "And did Mary's growing up pretty work out the way you thought it would?"

Mr. Kennicott brought his mind back from wherever it had gone. "Well, no. Not exactly." He chuckled. He had a nice chuckle, low and amused. He was a nice man. "Oh, the other boys began noticing Mary all right, but they didn't seem to make much headway with her. Once in a while she'd go to the movies with one of them, if Jack was off somewhere playing basketball or something. But it didn't mean anything. As for Jack, he never looked at another girl in his life, although if you come right down to it, I don't suppose he really thought of Mary as a girl. Most kids, when they get into High School, go through a girl-crazy stage, but Jack never did. He's a nice-looking boy, if I do say it as shouldn't, big and handsome with a wide grin—takes after his mother in looks—and he's got a nice way with him, too. Mannerly. Ma saw to that. He played on all the school teams and he was pretty good in his studies, too. I don't want to brag, but he's a boy any parent could be proud of, and I am proud of him." He laughed apologetically.

"I've been telling you about Mary, and how popular with the boys she got to be in High School. Well, the same thing goes for Jack. Being good-looking and captain of the football team, the girls chased after him something terrible. One spell there, Ma threatened to have the telephone taken out, the way it rang all the time with some girl calling up to say she'd lost her assignment book and would Jack please tell her what geometry problems they were supposed to do. He never caught on, either. It wasn't that he's dumb. He isn't. He was just so busy with one thing or another—sports, and studies, and an old car he rebuilt, and hunting and fishing—he was just so busy he didn't have time to think about girls. He was always polite enough to them, but his mind was on other things. Mostly they were things Mary was mixed up in, and I don't wonder he never thought of her as a girl. That jallopy, for instance. When he couldn't raise the price of a new set of spark plugs, she'd chip in and then they'd change them together. She knows as much about a Ford motor as most garage mechanics. Many's the time I've seen her, grease from head to foot, taking up the brakes or fiddling with the timing. When he wasn't using it, she'd use it; and when he graduated from High School and went into the Army, he gave it to her. That was a year and a half ago, when he was eighteen.

"First leave he had, Mary skipped school—she was a year

behind him—and spent the whole morning getting that jallopy tuned up. She and Ma went down to the station in it to meet the train, since I was at work and Ma don't drive. Ma told me about it later. Time had got away from Mary, so she hadn't had a chance to so much as wash her face, and she had on a pair of overalls, covered with oil. It didn't make any difference to her, nor to Jack. He jumped off the train, hugged his mother, and said to Mary, 'How's she running? Have you changed the oil yet?' Mary said, 'Yup. Gee, Jack, I'm glad you're home! There's something wrong with the wiring. We're getting a short.' As far as Ma could see, they started right in where they'd left off, and I guess that's the way it seemed to them, too. Except for Jack's being in uniform and not being in school, things were exactly the way they had been for the past ten or twelve years. Jack would go down-town and hang around the stores visiting with his old friends mornings, but he was back by the time Mary got out of school. Once in a while he'd bring her home in the jallopy, but only if he happened to be in that neighborhood. Then he'd go over and wait while she ate her lunch, or sometimes she'd come into our kitchen after she'd changed out of her school clothes into pants and make herself a sandwich to eat while they decided what to do that afternoon. It was like old times. Mary's mother said as much to Ma. 'Carrie,' she said, 'seems good to have Jack home, like old times, when we used to wonder which child belonged to who.' We always joked about that, because it always did seem as though both of them belonged to both families. You see, neither one of them had any brothers or sisters, and I suppose that made them closer than lots of next-door neighbors.

"Well, things went along about as usual until last June. The kids wrote to each other. Mary used to pass the letters she got from Jack around. No reason why she shouldn't. He'd ask questions about the families and the folks he knew. Once he wrote a whole letter about painting the boat and having the outboard overhauled. He and she'd built the boat together and they were pretty proud of it. It's the boat they're using now—not very big, so's they could carry it around to different lakes on a trailer they patched up, but a nice tight little boat, for all that. It wasn't what anyone could call a romantic correspondence, by any stretch of the imagination. Then June came, and Mary was all set to graduate. The Friday before graduation was the Senior Ball, and that's a big affair in our town, about the biggest of the year. For one thing, it's the only dance except the Elks' Easter Ball that everybody really dresses up for. The men and boys wear their good dark suits and the girls wear long dresses."

I knew how it was because it is the same in all rural communities. None of the men own evening clothes—such an extravagance would never occur to them; what's the sense of spending good money on an outfit you can wear only once or twice a year? But the girls and women do usually have one long dress, which they often make themselves and which they wear when occasion arises for several years, changing its appearance from time to time by altering the neckline or hem, or by dyeing it and adding a corsage of artificial flowers. Since it is the custom of the country to attend the ordinary run-of-the-mill dances in whatever you happen to have on when the notion to go hits you—polo shirts and corduroys, cotton dresses, pleated skirts and sweaters, anything—the unusual spectacle of a solid front of decent dark suits, with matching trousers and jackets, and of trailing skirts and bare arms creates a very gala and formal effect. People not only look different, but they act differently, so that the whole atmosphere surrounding the event is very special.

"Jack not being at home," Mr. Kennicott went on, "Mary went to the dance with Steve Proctor. Naturally she didn't want to miss it, it being one of the big events of her whole High School career, as you might say. I don't know why she picked Steve, specially, out of the herd, except maybe because all the girls were after him and it was sort of a feather in her cap that he asked her. You know how young girls are about things like that, even Mary, who is more sensible than most. Steve's all right—well-raised and all. Only thing wrong with him is maybe he's always had a little too much money and he's a little too handsome. That's a combination that can spoil any boy, and I guess Steve's done pretty well not to be any more spoiled than he is. He did things up brown for Mary— sent her flowers to wear and called for her in the new convertible his folks had managed to get somehow in spite of the war for his graduation present. We saw the whole performance out our living room window, with him handing her into the car like she was spun glass, and walking around to the driver's seat after tucking her skirt in and closing the door for her. Ma had to laugh, it was so different from when she went places with Jack. Then she has to swarm in the best she can under her own power, usually over the door which got jammed somehow and won't open, and more than half the time with the jallopy already under way. She can do it, too, neat as a cat; although I must say she took to Steve's methods like a duck takes to water. That's the woman of it for you."

He looked at me sideways, but I refused to rise to the bait.

"Along about ten o'clock, when Ma and I were just about

ready to turn off the radio and call it a day, someone ran up the steps and across the porch. Ma said, 'Land of Mercy, here's Jack!' and sure enough it was. He'd got leave unexpected and hitch-hiked home to surprise us. Ma bustled around getting him something to eat, and he said he guessed he'd call up Mary, since the lights were still on next door, and ask her over for a bite. So we told him where she was, and he said, 'Oh, sure. Did she get the boat painted, do you know?' We sat around talking and drinking Cokes for an hour or so, and then we started thinking about bed again. Just as we were all in the front hall, a car door slammed out front and someone came running up the walk. We stepped out and saw that it was Mary. 'Oh, Jack,' she said, 'someone at the dance said they saw you get out of a truck down on Main Street, and Steve wouldn't bring me home to see, so I swiped his car and I guess he's going to be mad, but I don't care; he can't push me around—' all in one breath and mixed up. Jack started to laugh, and then he got a good look at her and stopped.

"He'd never seen her in a long dress before. Maybe he'd never really seen her at all before. She sure was worth looking at. The dress was white with a great full skirt that made her waist look about six inches around, where it was tied with a silver ribbon. It was sort of old-fashioned around the top, like it was falling off her shoulders, only it was supposed to be that way. She was so tanned that her neck and shoulders looked dark against all that white and it gave her a look—glamorous, maybe you'd call it, or exotic. She was mad and excited, so her eyes snapped and her color was high, almost as bright as the flowers in her hair. She looked—well, beautiful. That's the only word for her. Jack just stood there, and then Steve Proctor came busting up the path. He was mad, too, and when you come right down to it, I don't know but what he had a right to be, with Mary running out on him and swiping his car to boot. He said, in that high-handed tone of his that always gets people's backs up, although I don't guess he means any harm, 'What's going on here? I don't appreciate having any girl of mine—'

"Mary looked at him and said, just as high and mighty as him, 'I'll have you understand I'm no girl of yours, Steve Proctor!' Then she turned her back on him and started up the steps toward Jack. I guess that's what did it, the way she came up those steps. With the women running around in short skirts and pants the way they do nowadays, you don't often get to see one of them go up steps the way my mother used to, bending and picking up her skirt just a little in front with both hands so she won't trip on it. I didn't know how much I'd missed it until I saw Mary do it, and then it occurred to me that it was one of the prettiest gestures a woman can make —graceful and womanly and—well, just plain pretty. I guess it struck Jack the same way. Next thing I knew, she was in his arms and he was hugging her as though he'd never let her go. He took time out to say over her head to Steve, 'Sorry, Bud, but Mary's my girl,' and then he kissed her.

"I'll say for Steve, he took it well, or maybe he knew when he was licked. He looked a little surprised, but then he laughed, not mad but real pleasant, and said, 'Okie-doke, my mistake.' Then he went and climbed into his car and drove away. About then Ma and I came to that we weren't needed, so we went back into the house.

"The kids wanted to get married right away, but we—her folks and Ma and me—persuaded them to wait till this fall. We were all so pleased, we wanted a bang-up wedding, and anyhow, they seemed so young. They're still pretty young, nineteen and twenty, but the way times are now, with Jack liable to be shipped overseas any day— So the wedding was a week ago last Friday, and it was real nice. Mary wore her Senior Ball dress—the one that caused all the trouble, if you want to put it that way—and her mother's veil, and with Jack in uniform they made a handsome couple. They'd always wanted to come up this way hunting, having heard a lot about the country, but of course it wasn't very feasible before they were married. So they planned this trip for their honeymoon. We joked about it a lot—seemed as if they were a lot more interested in getting their gear together for this trip than they were in the details of the wedding. If Mary's mother would have let her, I'll bet she'd have been perfectly satisfied to be married in her hunting clothes, so's not to delay starting up-country by having to change. They had the boat all loaded on the trailer the night before, and their duffle packed, and as soon as the reception was over, they struck north. That was the last we saw of them, waving and laughing in the old jallopy, with the trailer bobbling along behind."

Fred Judkin took up the tale. "They pulled into Durkee's along the early part of the afternoon. True helped them get their boat into the water, and showed them where they could leave the car, out of the way. The last he saw of them, they were headed down the Cambridge, following the channel stakes the way he told them. Of course, he couldn't see them much beyond Lakeside. The river takes a big bend there before it empties into Umbagog. But they were going along fine, as long as he could see them. They had plenty of daylight left so they should have made any camp site on the lake they saw fit, that night." He yawned. "It's past my bedtime. We want to get an early start to-morrow and cover some of the places we missed to-day." He got to his feet slowly and the rest of us followed suit. I said I'd have breakfast ready by six-thirty, so they could be on their way, and showed them where to sleep.

"Thank you for telling us about your son and his wife," I said to Mr. Kennicott. "They sound swell. I'm sure they're all right. Sleep well, and try not to worry."

His voice came back strong and confident. "Oh, I shall. I'm sure they're all right, too."

That was one of the noisy nights we sometimes get in the woods. Sometimes the wind can blow a gale, and all we hear is a distant roaring in the tree-tops and an occasional faint, faraway report as a fir-top snaps. At other times, as on that night, when the wind is in the right quarter, it kicks up a terrific clatter. It rattled shutters and riffled the shingles, sounding like a great beast clawing to get through the roof, sloping so close over our heads. The trees near the house tossed and groaned, and branches crashed to the ground. Sometime after midnight the wind went down and a still cold set in, making the timbers of the house creak and snap as they contracted. Used as I am to the woods and all its moods, I didn't sleep very well. I kept thinking of that boy and girl somewhere out in the vast night. They weren't just a couple of lost hunters to me any more, just a couple of nameless, faceless strangers who were no responsibility of mine. I knew them now, and so I worried about them. Supposing it were Rufus or Dinah? I abandoned that line quickly. It wouldn't bear thinking on, so I thought of Mr. Kennicott instead. If I were worried, what must he be going through, now that he was alone, without the barrier of human speech and companionship to stand between him and the cold, logical doubts that pounce in the night? I was glad when the window showed gray, and I could get up and build the fire and start breakfast.

I was still alone when Mr. Kennicott came into the kitchen. Last night he'd looked old and tired and troubled, but this morning his face was as gray and composed as stone. I showed him where he could wash and gave him a clean towel, and he thanked me. Then he said calmly, "I've made up my mind that my boy is dead."

"Oh, no!" I protested. "No!" I couldn't bear to think that the laughing, ardent boy and girl whom I had met the night before were not living and laughing still somewhere near to us.

"Yes. I guess I've known it all along, but I wouldn't let myself believe it. During the night I saw there was no use in trying to run away from it any longer. I appreciate your sympathy, Mrs. Rich, but I'm certain. I've had all night to think, and now I'm—reconciled." The last word was almost inaudible, weighted as it was with sorrow; and now I didn't see how I could bear the knowledge of this man's bitter cup, which he must accept and drink alone, among strangers. We heard Ralph and Fred thumping down the stairs, and Mr. Kennicott added quickly, "No need of upsetting them. I ought not to have told you—only you seemed so interested last night in the children." I guess it was his using the word "children" for the first time in all our talk that illogically convinced me that his intuition was not playing him false. Then his tone became almost brisk as the others entered the room. "Starting to spit a little snow. We've got no time to waste." I looked out the window and saw the first fine flakes which presage a serious storm slanting down against the black wall of the forest across the river.

I shall never forget that breakfast. You don't ever forget an overwhelming demonstration of the incredible extent of human fortitude. No one would have suspected, unless like me he knew, down what bleak prospect those mild eyes were gazing as Mr. Kennicott drank his orange juice. His obedient fingers handled knife and fork without a tremor as he ate his bacon and eggs. He made an observation or two about the weather and the war; he answered comments naturally, giving his full and tranquil attention to the speaker; once he even laughed. I do not know, I cannot imagine, upon what secret reservoir of strength he was drawing, nor can I comprehend the extent of a natural dignity and consideration that forbade, even under those Spartan circumstances, making others uncomfortable by a parade of grief. He seemed just an ordinary man, heroic in neither appearance nor manner; but I learned then that Courage sometimes chooses just such a simple face to wear.

Over the last cups of coffee, he and Fred discussed their program for the day. They had planned to go back the way they had come, covering that part of the shore of Umbagog that they had missed by taking the short-cut the day before. But the snow was making on the ground so fast by that time that the sensible course was obvious: to abandon the idea of scrambling over the fifteen miles or so of icy rocks which comprise the shoreline, and to take the more direct and sheltered B Pond Trail to Upton. Then they would surely get back before traveling became impossible. Fred and Ralph went back upstairs to put their boots on, and I started slapping together a few sandwiches for them to take with them. Mr.

Kennicott finished his coffee, and then he asked me rather diffidently how much he owed me for the lodging and meals.

I was surprised, and a little hurt, so I spoke more abruptly than I intended to. "Why, nothing. Do you think we'd take money for helping people in trouble? We've had our troubles, too, when we've had to accept help, and the least we can do is help others—" I broke off, ashamed of myself. I was afraid I sounded a little smug, and anyhow, the occasion didn't call for a stump speech from me.

He said simply, "Thank you," and then Ralph and Fred came back. In a few minutes the three of them started out of the yard, heads bent against the blowing snow, because Ralph thought he knew where there was a piece of angle-iron for Cliff in a deserted shack over by B Pond, and this was a good time to go and see. I had just turned away from the window when the telephone emitted Joe's distinctive ring.

"Hello, Louise," he said. "Trouble, trouble, trouble. Now we've lost Fred Judkin and that boy's father, Kennicott. You haven't seen anything of them?"

I said that I had indeed, and that they were already on their way home.

"Well, thank God for that, anyhow," he commented piously. "Things are bad enough already. Louise, they just found the boat that young couple set out in, all stove up on the shore opposite Big Island. Guess there's no doubt but what they're at the bottom of Umbagog. Judging from where the boat was found, they couldn't have any more than got started when they swamped or capsized. It's too bad, a young couple like that."

"But maybe they got ashore, Joe. Maybe they're trying to find their way—"

"I'm afraid not. Where they found the boat wasn't more'n half an hour's walk through the woods to Durkee's, and if they swam ashore to the New Hampshire side, they'd have landed right in front of Mrs. Potter's. She's gone South, but her farmer's still there. I guess they're drowned all right."

"But, Joe, Mr. Kennicott said they both were wonderful swimmers, and it was a seaworthy little boat."

He sighed. "Louise, you'd ought to know by now that no one can swim ten strokes in these lakes in November, specially in the kind of clothes you have to wear at this time of year to keep from freezing to death. Like as not they had high boots on, along with heavy coats and pants." I did know it, of course. The water is paralyzingly cold, just above the freezing point. "And about the boat—boats that are all right in other lakes, aren't all right in Umbagog. You know that, too, or you'd ought to. That's a mean lake." I was still silent, because everything he said was perfectly true, and too many people had already been drowned in Umbagog for ignoring those facts. Joe went on, "What they figure happened, they were going along all right until after they got past Davis Landing. It's sheltered in there, and they didn't realize how rough it was until they come out into the main lake, there by Potter's. Then it was too late. They've got a party going out this morning to drag for the bodies, but I don't think there's much hope of finding them till spring. The lake will be froze over in a couple of days, soon as we get a still night. It's too bad. Why, they couldn't have been married more'n two-three hours."

"But, Joe, why didn't they find the boat before, if it was so near Upton?"

"It was too near. No one thought anything could have happened to them so quick, so they all started searching farther afield."

I hung up, feeling that most futile of all emotions, rebellious anger at the lack of discrimination shown by Death. With all the people in the world who wanted to die, who were better off dead, or who deserved to die, why did it have to be these? It was so stupid. It was so wasteful. There was nothing either original or constructive about these reflections, and I knew it, but that didn't prevent me from indulging in them. I was working myself up into a fine frenzy when a knock on the door brought me up short. I opened it to find Mr. Kennicott, his cap and shoulders powdered white, standing there in the falling snow.

"I had to come back," he said. "I got to thinking about you feeling so bad. Don't. The way I look at it, you go when your time comes, and their time had come. If it had to happen, it couldn't have happened better. Really it couldn't, Mrs. Rich. They were head-over-heels in love, and they were together, the way they wanted to be, looking forward to life. If they'd lived, maybe they'd never have been so happy again. Likely things wouldn't have been anywhere near as wonderful as they planned. Life never is. Things go wrong. At least they'll never have to go through what Ma and me and her folks have been through in these last three days." He hesitated, trying to think of something more to say, but there wasn't anything more; so he turned half-away. "Just don't feel so bad, Mrs. Rich."

I promised that I'd try not to. It never occurred to me to tell him about Joe's call. He knew the truth already, and he'd made his own terms with it. We said good-bye again, and he hurried off after the others. After he was out of sight, I closed the door slowly, thinking about what he had said. There was a lot of truth in it, I thought; but mostly I thought about Mr. Kennicott's taking the trouble, burdened as he was, to come way back to say a few words of comfort to a woman he'd never seen before and would never see again. The dead boy had been cheated out of something a lot more valuable than the few short hours of happiness which had been Life's final gift to him. The real tragedy was that now he'd never have the chance to grow, to develop through living and suffering, into the kind and gentle man his father was.

7

Rienza Trimback

HERE IN THE backcountry, a far larger percentage of women are married than in urban areas. This is, I believe, because neither men nor women get along very well here alone. In the first place, there are very few lines of endeavor in which a woman can support herself. Almost the only job she can get, unless she is trained to teach school, is keeping house for a widower with children, and then she usually ends by marrying him. In order to eat, a girl either has to marry or move away to some town or city where opportunities for women are more varied and numerous. In the few cases where a woman inherits enough property to live on, she still needs a man around the place. It's a rare woman who can shingle the barn roof or plow the back pasture herself; and the hiring of occasional help isn't too satisfactory. It always turns out that on the three days when she really needs someone to put up the hay for her, every man in the community is busy in his own hay fields; and on the fourth, it rains.

This is not a one-sided proposition. A man needs a woman to look after him, too. There are no convenient restaurants where he can get his meals, no laundries with mending service to take care of his clothes, no women-by-the-day to clean up his house, no Visiting Nurse to tend him when he is sick. A man alone is a pretty sad object in the country, with buttons dangling, pants held up with safety pins, the lean and hungry look that comes of a diet of fried foods, and a neglected house where the beds are never made and no flowers grow in the dooryard or on the kitchen window sills.

This doesn't mean that country marriages are simply marriages of convenience. In the country more than anywhere else marriage includes true companionship, based not only on mutual dependence in material matters, but in matters of the mind and spirit as well. Here where in winter the countryside is so bleak and white that even the roofs look lonely, where for days, sometimes, a farm is cut off from the world by drifted roads, the society of another human being whose aims and interests and affections are one's own is a constant and necessary bulwark against the forces of loneliness and despair. Marriage here is the natural state, an axiom of satisfactory living, and it is a rare person who is not married by the time he or she reaches the upper twenties. Exceptions do occur, and Rienza Trimback is one of them. Her story, with no important differences, is the story of almost every unmarried woman hereabouts.

We have, as my more worldly friends often point out to me, some peculiar names in Maine. I like them myself, the names like Laurel and Ivy and Maple and Fern, bestowed through a love of the green growing things. I like the biblical names—Bathsheba, Serepta, Joshua, and Nahum. Some of the names are old-fashioned and prim, like Prudence and Araminta and Charity, and some of them are just made up and fanciful, designed, I suppose, to bring beauty and poetry to a Spartan existence—Lunetta, Velzora, Jolene. I know one young man who was named for a can of peaches. His mother, wracking her brains for a name for the new baby, happened to see the can on the kitchen shelf, so his name is Delmonte. Then there are the names that were originally brought home from the far places of the earth by sea-faring ancestors and handed down from generation to generation, so that to-day I know a Persia, a Casindania, a Ceylon, and, of course, Rienza Trimback.

Rienza Trimback was a very attractive girl forty-odd years ago, when she was eighteen. I've seen pictures of her and I've heard people talk about her. The pictures show a girl with dark eyes, wide with innocent question, over a mouth, large and sweet, that seems disciplined with difficulty into gravity. Her dark hair is swept up into a pompadour that leaves bare the broad serene forehead and little, close-set ears. Her chin is round and young, and she's a pretty thing, with the unfinished, soft prettiness of youth.

"The good times I used to have with Rienza!" one great-grandmother who was a girl with her told me, shaking her head and smiling. "Didn't take anything to set us off in them days. Giggle, giggle, giggle from morning till night. It got so our mothers wouldn't let us set together in church, we behaved so unseemly. Not that we meant any harm or disrespect to the minister, but you know how young girls are. We found a tee-hee's nest in every ha-ha bush. That girl could dance the shoes off the devil himself. That was when I was engaged to Oren, and she was runnin' 'round with Barrett Ames. There wasn't a dance within thirty miles that we didn't take in. We had an awful good time. She might have married Barry, too—although I dunno; she had a drove of them after her, and could have taken her pick of half a dozen—only that winter, when she was goin' on nineteen—"

The winter when Rienza was almost nineteen, her mother caught cold on the way home from a funeral and was dead of pneumonia within the week. Pneumonia took a terrific toll in those days, when a doctor was seldom called until the patient was desperately ill, and sometimes, overworked, exhausted, delayed by bad roads, couldn't get there until the day after that, when it would have been too late even had he had modern drugs to rely upon; and one funeral, with the long committal service in a barren and sleet-swept graveyard, was all too frequently closely followed by at least one other. Rienza's mother was a victim of the times; and so, no less, was Rienza. She was the youngest of nine children and the only unmarried girl in the family, so it was taken for granted that she would be the one to stay at home and keep house for her father. She didn't rebel against the edict of her brothers and sisters and the neighbors. Probably there wasn't any edict, when it comes to that. She simply fell into the accepted pattern of the day. If a man had an unmarried daughter, naturally she looked after him, if his wife died. It was her duty.

Rienza's father, old Ephraim Trimback, had been ailing vaguely ever since he'd fallen out of a haymow a year or two before, and after the blow of the death of his wife, he began to fail visibly. The consensus was that he wasn't long for this world. Three or four years would see Rienza free to live her own life, everybody said, and what a comfort it would be to her in after years to know that she had done her duty well. It was wonderful, they all said, how a flibbertigibbet like she'd always been could settle down in the traces. She was turning out to be as good a housekeeper as her mother had been before her, and that was saying a lot. She kept a big flock of hens herself, for the egg money, and her married brothers came over regularly to help her father with the heavy chores. It was a very good arrangement all around. Of course, during the period of mourning for her mother she couldn't attend any public gathering except church, and some of the young men who had been attentive to her drifted away to other girls, who were free to go dancing and sleigh-riding. But Clyde Matthews and Barrett Ames and Wilbur Pottle remained faithful, even if it did mean spending long evenings talking to old Eph. Confined to the farmhouse by his respect for convention and what was becoming semi-invalidism, he developed a thirst for sociability and a tendency to monopolize Rienza's callers.

When the conventional year was over, Rienza prepared to resume her own social life. She'd agreed to go to the Valentine Day dance in Bethel with Clyde, and she was looking forward to it eagerly. It seemed a long time since she'd danced. She altered her last year's flowered challis, which she'd had little occasion to wear, and washed her hair and brushed it until it shone. She looked very pretty when Clyde called for her, with her eyes sparkling and her cheeks flushed with excitement. She put on her coat and turned to say good-night to her father.

"Now don't you wait up for me, Pa," she admonished him. "You go to bed when you get ready. I won't be very late."

"Have a good time," he said. He gave a slight grimace of pain. "I—I guess I'll go to bed now. I don't seem to feel very spry. No, no, don't you bother none about me. I'll be all right. Just you go along and have a good time."

That time she went, but of course she didn't have a good time. She couldn't help worrying about her father, alone and sick, and long before the dance was over, she told Clyde that she was terribly sorry, but she thought that she ought to go home. He was very nice and understanding about it, even after they discovered when they got back to the Trimback place that old Eph was sleeping the sleep commonly accredited to the just, after having, from the evidence, disposed of a glass or two of milk and almost half a mince pie. But the same thing happened again and again, until it became apparent to everyone except Rienza that her father simply didn't want her to go anywhere. Whether this was just because he was lonely without her, or because of a deeper-seated fear that she would marry and upset his well-established way of life, there is no way of knowing. Whatever the case, no sooner would she start getting ready to go out than he would develop a symptom.

"Gol-ram it, Rienza," he'd moan, "my back's killin' me. Don't seems if I can stand it. Maybe a hot soap stone—" And she'd drop everything to build up the kitchen fire and heat the stone and get him into bed.

Or he'd say, "By Jim Hill, Rienza, I knew when I et them beans you'd sneaked some mustard in. You know I can't stomach mustard, an' now I got the cramps. Gol-ram it, can't you do nothin' for me? Stir up some ginger tea or sompthin'?" Eph Trimback was a very religious man. He'd been a deacon of the church in his better days, and no more violent oath than Gol-ram or Jim Hill was ever heard to cross his lips. He could put a lot of feeling into those innocuous expressions, though. They never left you in any doubt as to his attitude toward anything that displeased him.

"To hear the old goat Gol-ramming and Jim-hilling around," Barrett Ames said bitterly one night down at the store, "you'd think he was dying and it was Rienza who was killing him." Barry was the only one left of Rienza's train of beaux. The others had become discouraged. He had been counting on taking her to the Strawberry Festival at the Grange that night, and his disappointment when she couldn't go because her father seemed to be suffering from the combined effects of food poisoning and galloping consumption had left him in a violent and outspoken mood. "There's nothing more the matter with him than there is with me, and probably not as much. He'll outlive the whole of us. It makes me mad, the way he puts it over on Rienza. What she'd ought to do is just walk out on him once or twice when he starts throwing a fit, and let him fend for himself. By the time she came home, he'd have got over what ailed him. But she won't. He's got her buffaloed."

Finally even he couldn't stand it any longer. He begged her to marry him and put an end to an impossible situation. "Your father could come and live with us," he said. "Or he could go live with one of your brothers or sisters. You've done your share. Let them do theirs."

"But, Barry, this is his home. He wouldn't be happy anywhere else. Besides, I couldn't ask my brothers to take him, even if he'd go. All the burden would fall on their wives, and that wouldn't be right. They're not blood kin. My sisters all have big families and more worry and expense already than—"

"Then board him out somewhere. I'd be willing to help pay—"

"I couldn't do that!" Rienza looked at him with shocked eyes. "My own father. I'm surprised that you'd suggest it. Oh, Barry, it isn't that I don't love you. I do, I do, more than I can say! But it would kill him to move, even to your place. If you could only see your way clear to come and live here, just until— We're young. We've got lots of time ahead of us."

"No." Barry was sure about that. "I feel the same way as he does about my own place, and I can't live anywhere that I'm not the boss. It wouldn't work out. Rienza, can't you *see?* You're only twenty-three, but I'm over thirty. I haven't got all the time in the world. He's had his life. It's only fair that he should step down now and let us have our chance!"

But Rienza couldn't see it. Her duty was her duty.

"All right. I guess that settles it. I won't be hanging around here any more, Rienza. I can stand only just so much, and I've reached the end of my tether. If you change your mind—"

Rienza didn't believe him, really, when he said he wouldn't be back. She kept expecting him for a long time, until at last she heard that he was taking Winona Frayle around to all the dances. Then it was too late to change her mind, even if she would. Barry married Winona five years after Rienza's mother died, and that was the year when people began to say that Rienza was starting to show her age. The round softness of her face changed, and her jawline began to show fine and firm. Her lips thinned a little and looked less ready to laugh, and her eyes took on a steadfastness. She wasn't pretty any longer, but there were those who thought she'd grown into a very handsome woman, handsomer than her young prettiness had promised.

One thing Barry had been wrong about. Old Eph didn't outlive them all. Under Rienza's excellent care, he outlasted his wife by fifteen years, and died at the age of eighty, of a heart attack. He left Rienza the farm and a little money, which everyone including her brothers and sisters agreed was only right, and the satisfaction of knowing that no one could possibly accuse her of dereliction. If she found that knowledge rather cold comfort sometimes, nobody ever suspected it. Rienza had never been one to complain.

She was thirty-four, which was pretty old for marriage in the country in those days, but the friends of her girlhood, all married and mothers by this time, undertook to find Rienza a nice beau and marry her off. All her old admirers were settled down, of course, but as one friend said, "There are plenty more fish in the sea." Their good offices weren't really necessary. Rienza was a good-looking woman with property of her own now. Pretty soon she had two eligible suitors calling on her. One was Lee Miller, a widower of forty with two small children and a farm of his own, and the other was the new minister, William Stoddard, a handsome man of about Rienza's age, and miraculously unmarried. Opinion was divided as to which was the more suitable. Some held that Rienza was farm born and bred, and ought to stick to a life that she knew. Others maintained that she was naturally high-minded and smart as a whip and would make a wonderful minister's wife. Her experience with the ill and elderly would come in handy, and she could make a lot of the pastoral calls and be a real help to her husband.

What she thought herself it was difficult to guess. At the Ladies' Aid chicken pie supper it was observed that she sat with Lee Miller and was perfectly lovely to his children, always a good sign. But when she and Mr. Stoddard were invited over to the Freeman Howards' for Thursday night boiled dinner, it came out in the conversation that she'd helped him with the Scott Evans funeral sermon which had been so well-thought-of by everyone. Of course, someone would have to help him, he being so new and all. He couldn't be expected to know about certain episodes in Scott's life to which it would have been unfortunate to make even accidental reference. But that he had chosen Rienza for this task was considered highly significant. She herself parried all questions and hints blandly. She agreed that the Miller young-ones ought to have a woman to take care of them, and in the next breath agreed that the Reverend was a fine man and should have a wife to help him in his work. Nobody got much change out of Rienza, as Winona Ames told Barrett, adding that in her opinion Rienza took a rather spiteful delight in keeping everyone on tenterhooks. Winona, after ten years of marriage to Barry, wasn't exactly jealous of Rienza, but she couldn't have been called precisely her kindest critic.

Which one she would have married—and almost certainly she would have married one or the other—it is impossible for anyone, probably even Rienza, to say at this late date. The matter was never settled. At the time when it might have been, Rienza's Aunt Martha suffered a stroke. Aunt Martha and Uncle Widd were childless, and it never occurred to anyone, least of all to Rienza herself, that she had done her share for the family. She was single; she was accustomed to taking care of older people; she was the obvious one to step into the breach. So she moved over to the next farm and undertook the nursing of her aunt and the housekeeping for her uncle.

At first she must have believed, or tried to believe, or hoped, at least, that the arrangement was only temporary, that Aunt Martha would get better or someone else would be found to take over the responsibility. She never said so to a living soul, but she took with her only a few of her clothes, and ran home across the fields and over the brook every day or so for something she hadn't thought she'd need. For a long time she took Thursday afternoons to herself, to go over to her own house

and tidy it up and air out the rooms. Occasionally she settled
Aunt Martha comfortably for several hours, prepared and
served an early supper for easygoing Uncle Widd, and went
over home, as she called it, to get ready a meal and entertain
her friends under her own roof. Sometimes she included Lee
Miller in these gatherings, and sometimes William Stoddard,
and sometimes both of them.

These evenings had little in common with the old laughing,
rollicking days when she had gone dancing with Barrett Ames.
They were all older and settled now, and married couples of
those days didn't attend dances and race over country roads
beneath the setting moon. There were the children to think
of, at home in the care of an obliging relative or neighbor who
didn't want to be kept up much later than ten o'clock; and the
countryman's day starts too early to make late hours attractive. After supper they usually played whist or fan-tan—for
matches, of course, or just for fun. When the game was over,
they drank sweet cider or lemonade and ate sugar cookies and
hermits, and talked for a few moments. Then someone said,
"Well, much as I hate to break up the party—"; and someone
else said, "Let me help you with these dishes, Rienza. The two
of us, it won't take any time at all." This offer was a courteous
gesture, and was always rejected with equal courtesy. "Oh,
my, no. There are only a few. It won't take me a minute—or I
might leave them till morning."

By ten o'clock the sedate party was over, the guests were
going down the steps, and the country stillness was broken
with "Had a *lovely* time, Rienza!" and "You come over to our
house next week," and, distance-diminished, "Good-night,
good-night!" Then Rienza would do up her dishes, and plump
up cushions, and put out lights; and if sometimes she dawdled

over these tasks, pretending that when they were done she would go up-stairs to her own bed, to a sleep untroubled by the necessity of keeping one ear alert for an invalid's call, no one ever knew. She'd go about the house one last time, twitching a curtain straight, lingering in the last heat of the stove; and then she'd put on her coat, lock the door behind her, and trudge off across the fields to where the light in Aunt Martha's window beckoned, her head held high, her shoulders square, denying herself the useless indulgence of a backward glance at the low white house sleeping in the starlight.

At the end of three years, William Stoddard received a call to a larger church. He talked with Rienza before he accepted it, asking, although he already knew what the answer must be, whether she wouldn't accompany him. She was truly fond of him—not with the headlong passion which she'd felt for Barry Ames, but with a maturer, quieter affection none the less genuine. But she couldn't go with him. God had appointed her to a post which she couldn't desert, she told him; and she couldn't urge him to stay, living in a hope which might never be realized, when he'd been summoned to a field of greater usefulness. It sounds like a stilted little speech for anyone as practical and down-to-earth as Rienza was, but it came from the bottom of her heart, and William Stoddard came away from the interview very much moved. Years later, after he'd married and become a successful city pastor, they still exchanged letters at Christmastime; and sometimes on Sunday afternoons—this was much later—she'd listen to his beautiful voice, trained and polished now, come in over her battery-operated radio, and wonder that she was so little affected by anything except a faint and natural curiosity as to how well she would have fitted into the life he had made for himself.

Not very well, she concluded, giving herself less credit than she deserved.

After the Reverend Stoddard went away, Lee Miller increased his attentions. Rienza liked him and she really loved his two little girls, who were being brought up more or less haphazardly by a series of Lee's female relations, who came and did for him and the children for as long or short periods as their own domestic arrangements would allow. Rienza realized that this was not an ideal, or even a very good, situation for two little girls approaching adolescence and its problems. Completely ignorant of modern psychiatry, she was nevertheless informed by her common sense that the girls lacked the emotional security and the consistent discipline and routine that were necessary to their welfare. That isn't the way she put it, the day she saw Saba, a precocious twelve-year-old, down at the store in lipstick and near-silk stockings, carrying on, as Rienza put·it, with one of the Barlow boys, who was seventeen if he was a day. Rienza, whom few things shocked any more, was shocked that day. She left her basket of groceries to be called for later and marched up the dirt road to the Miller farm, heedless alike of the dust raised by her determined progress and of the hot July sun beating down on her bare head. Lee was hoeing in his bean field, and she summoned him to the wall with a shout and an imperative wave of the arm. She wasted no time on the amenities.

"Lee, if you don't do something pretty quick about those girls of yours, the first thing you know they're going to get into about the worst kind of trouble a girl can get into. I guess you know what I mean without my saying any more about that, but I'm too fond of them and of you to let them go the way they're going without at least having my say-so. I don't know what in tunket your sister Liz is thinking of to let a child like Saba rig herself up the way I just saw her down to the store, but—"

"Whoa-back, Rienza," Lee said in understandable bewilderment. "What's biting you? You seem a little up-sot."

"I am up-set. When I see a nice child that I've known from the cradle rolling her eyes and batting her lashes and swinging her hips at a man old enough to be her father, like a—a—well, a movie star, I figure I've got a right to be up-set. What Liz—"

"Now wait. Let's get this straight. In the first place, Liz had to go home yesterday. Her mother-in-law's sick. My cousin Fawnie'll come over from Sumner as soon's her oldest girl gets back from Boston, and—"

"That's just what I'm talking about. What kind of a way for those poor young-ones to live is that? Never knowing who's going to be bossing them from one day to the next, having to change their ideas and their habits every ten minutes— Yesterday Liz, who's a wonderful woman, I'll grant you, but inclined to be a little bit too strict; and to-morrow Fawnie, who I must say, much as I like her, is downright slack about a lot of things. When I think—"

"Now wait." Lee was a patient and methodical man. "Let's get back to the store. Who's this man old enough to be her father that Saba's flirting with?"

"Maybe I did exaggerate that a little. It was Wade Barlow, and if he isn't old enough to be her father, he's a lot too old for her to be fooling with, even if it's only in fun. I wouldn't trust those Barlow boys as far as I could throw them, but this time I will say that it's not all his fault. Saba may be only twelve, but got up the way she is, with silk stockings and lipstick and a tight dress, she looks older and—"

"Lipstick? I don't know anything about any lipstick and silk stockings. Where'd she get those?"

"How do I know where she got them? That's what I'm trying to tell you. You ought to have a woman in the house that'll look after those girls. They're good girls, but they're getting to the silly age. I know all about it. I was that age once myself." She stopped short, looking comically startled. "If you can believe it," she added dryly. "But that's not the point. The point is that they haven't got anyone to tell them things. No man, no matter how hard he tries—and you do try, Lee; you're a good father—can bring up two girls alone. What you'd ought to do is get married to a nice, good-hearted, sensible woman. There." She folded her arms and scowled at him.

Lee straightened up and shoved his broad-brimmed straw hat onto the back of his head. "I'm glad you brought it out into the open, Rienza. I been trying to work up to it gradual for the past couple of years, but I never seem to be able to find the right time to ask you. You'd be pretty near perfect, and I guess you know I think the world and all of you."

"That wasn't what I was leading up to at all. You know I can't marry anybody, with Aunt Martha the way she is, getting more helpless all the time and no telling how long it'll last. I've given up any idea of ever marrying." The minute she said it, she knew it was true, had been true for quite a while, although never before had she faced it, and right now she was too busy and concerned to spare any time indulging in regret that it should be so. "You're a good man, an awful good man, and if things were different, I'd be pleased to— But there's no use in thinking about that. No use at all." She had a sudden tired feeling that she'd been through this too many times before, and that the sooner it was over, the better.

"You've got to pick out someone else that's suitable and just go ahead and marry her."

"Sounds easy," Lee commented with mild cynicism.

"Well, it is easy. Any woman in her right mind would be glad to marry you, if you'd just get up enough gumption to go after her."

"I'm interested to hear it," said Lee, and added with humorous intent: "And I suppose you've got her all picked out for me."

"Since you mention it, yes, I have." Rienza recognized the humor but decided to ignore it; this was too good an opportunity to waste. "Marge Abbott. She's a widow with no children of her own, and she's good with young-ones or she wouldn't be such a successful schoolteacher. She's just about the right age, and she's nice-looking and capable. Besides, I've seen her casting sheep's eyes at you—"

The next day she started closing up her own house, which had stood ready for immediate occupancy for five years. She took down the curtains and washed them and put them away in bureau drawers. She aired and sunned the blankets and quilts and packed them in trunks, with cedar boughs to keep out moths. She rolled up the rugs, and turned the mattresses over the foots of the beds, and oiled the stoves against rust, and spread newspapers over the parlor carpet, and pulled all the shades down to the window sills, and disconnected the pump. Then she turned the key in the kitchen door, and picked up the bushel basket of odds and ends, such as the egg-beater that was better than Aunt Martha's and the iron gem pans to which she attributed her fame as a maker of pop-overs, and went once more across the fields and over the brook to Uncle Widd's, with the dead house staring at her inflexible back from blind eyes.

It was at about this time that she began to acquire her reputation for being—well, not exactly queer, but for sometimes doing odd and unaccountable things, like walking alone on stormy nights when all sensible folk were safely and warmly housed. She herself couldn't have explained why she did it. She'd stand in the window, listening to the wind pour over the house and away across the pastures, thinking how far it had come and how far it was going. She'd think of the things it had seen, the lakes and mountains to the north, the endless stretches of forest where rabbit and wildcat and deer felt its lash, and suddenly she'd feel that she couldn't tolerate being shut away here, behind glass, a moment longer. She'd snatch her coat and rush out to walk swiftly, head lifted and long back straight, over the empty wind-washed fields and roads. "Her age," her friends said wisely. "Old maids of a certain age get notions." But it wasn't her age that sometimes gave her the trapped feeling that forced her to stride the open countryside with only the friendly wind for company.

At about this time, too, people began to notice that Rienza's speech and manner, which had always been tactful and ladylike, were undergoing a change. She was always pleasant still, but people began to say that you'd better not ask Rienza's opinion unless you were prepared to hear exactly what she thought, expressed in plain terms. It wasn't that she was ever rude. It was more as if she had decided that, while she was clearing her life of unessentials like the care of a house she never used and the attentions of men she could never marry, she might as well make a clean sweep and throw overboard all the affectations and poses to which she had been trained.

And eight months after her interview with him, Lee Miller and Marge Abbott were married. It turned out very well, too. Aunt Martha died about four years later, but of course Uncle Widd still needed someone to do for him, especially now that his arthritis was getting so bad; so Rienza stayed on. The amount of housework involved didn't fill her time, so she increased her flock and started raising fancy poultry and eggs for market. The farm was not at all isolated now that most roads were hard-surfaced and everyone had cars, and she had a good business established by the time Uncle Widd died. He left her his farm and eight thousand dollars in the bank, which is quite a lot of money by local standards.

For the first time in her adult life, Rienza was free of responsibility. She was fifty-five years old, financially independent—what is known here as very well-fixed—and a good-looking woman for her age or any other age, for that matter. There was quite a lot of gray in her hair, but her eyes looked bigger and darker than ever since her face had grown thinner. Her figure and erect carriage were the envy of her friends, who had to a woman paid the price of child-bearing and hard work. Not that Rienza didn't work hard. She did. She enlarged her poultry farm to include much of Uncle Widd's land, moved back to her own house, and took advantage of the times and easier transportation to rent Uncle Widd's house to a man with a family, who worked in the mills in Rumford. He only wanted enough land for a garden, so it was a good deal for her. She began selling her poultry and eggs to wholesalers who called for them twice a week in trucks, and before long she was adding to Uncle Widd's bank account instead of living on it. Oh, yes, she worked hard, but it was the strenuous kind of outdoor work that kept her slim and brown. She appeared at the store one day in dungarees and a work shirt, and the disapproving comment was that from the back you could hardly tell her from one of those young summer women. Usually, though, she didn't wear her work clothes off the farm, and that one lapse was forgiven her when Winona Ames died of influenza and, after a decent interval, Barrett began calling on her, taking up, as one commentator put it, right where he'd left off thirty years before.

There was something right about this second flowering of the old romance, something fitting about the completion of the interrupted cycle, that appealed to the drama-starved hearts of the country people. To a man and woman they were pleased and gratified, and they did everything in their power to nurture the affair. "It's nice after all this time that they should get together at last. Just like a movie. Let's have them over for Sunday dinner," or "Makes you feel things are planned. Here she's stayed single all these years, and he's alone now, with his young-ones all married off. I'm plannin' on makin' a crocheted pop-corn spread for her a weddin' present."

But the Sunday chicken was slaughtered in vain and the pop-corn spread went to the maker's granddaughter when she married, because for some reason the romance failed to mature. Rienza scandalized the neighbors by having her hair cut and buying a station wagon and a pedigreed police dog, and Barry's second son and his wife took over the Ames place and made a home for Barry. Nobody could understand it at all, and it's only by luck that I do. Larry Parsons was buying the considerable amounts of eggs and poultry required in the hotel business from Rienza, and one day when I was riding to Rumford with him on business, we went around by the Trimback place to pick up some crates of eggs.

Rienza was dressing broilers in the woodshed when we drove into the yard, and came out to meet us, tall and lithe in her dungarees, her short gray hair curling close to her beautifully shaped head, and her fine lean face as keen as a hawk's. "Oh, it's only you," she said to Larry. "Though I don't know what difference it would make who it was. I'd look just the same. Times have changed since I was a girl. My mother always wore four aprons, one on top of another, and when the doorbell rang she'd send one of us young-ones to peek before she'd answer the door. If 'twas only one of the neighbors, she'd just take off the top apron, which was made of flour sacking that she wouldn't be caught dead in by anyone, and go to the door in the second apron, which was clean, but maybe faded or patched. If 'twas someone she didn't know quite so well, she'd take that off and go in the one underneath, which was bright and new, but still only percale or calico. But if 'twas a stranger or the minister, she'd peel down to the last one, one of these dress-up aprons, pretty as could be, but only half as big as a handkerchief and no earthly use except for decoration. But I can't very well take these pants off—or at least, I can, but I'm not going to. There's enough talk about me already without my throwing kerosene on the flame."

"Now what've you been doing?" Larry wanted to know.

"Nothing," she stated vigorously. "Not one darned thing, unless you count having a new bathroom put in, with a shower in it. It's the shower that sticks in their craws, I guess. Unwomanly. But I've always read about showers and thought I'd like one. I do, too, and since I earned the money that paid for it, I don't see how anyone's got any call to kick. Then of course I've been talking about hiring that G.I. and his wife that live in Uncle Widd's house to tend the chickens a couple of months this winter, so I can go to Florida. I'm going to do it, too. Might even take him into the business, if he pans out all right. But of course the talk all goes back eight-nine years to when I didn't marry Barrett Ames after all. That's at the bottom of it all."

"Why didn't you marry him, Rienza?" Larry asked. "I've often wondered." It wasn't an impertinent question. There was something so frank and friendly and sensible about the woman that even I, who didn't know her, would have felt free to ask her almost anything, knowing that if she didn't want to tell me, she'd say so with perfect good nature.

"Well, I almost did. At my age you don't fall madly in love all over again, but I'd always been awful fond of Barry. I still am. I was sick and tired of paddling my own canoe all those years, and he looked like a nice strong shoulder to lean on. You must know how 'tis, Mrs. Rich, you being a widow with small children," she said to me. "Don't you sometimes feel like you'd give anything to have someone else decide things for you?"

I said I did indeed.

"There's worse things than having to stand on your own two feet," she warned me. "But like I was saying, I'd pretty near made up my mind to marry Barry, when one day I noticed the way he got up out of a low chair, easy and careful, for all the world like Uncle Widd used to, and my father before him. It came to me then that Barry is twelve years older than I am, and while he was hale and hearty then, 'twouldn't be long before he was an old man. I've spent my entire life seeing old people through their last illnesses—not that I'm complaining—and I decided that I'd had enough of it. I missed my youth, if you want to call it that, and marrying Barry or anyone else wouldn't bring it back. I'd got along single for fifty-six years, and I decided I might as well tough it out to the end."

"Don't you ever get lonesome?" I asked out of my own experience.

"Of course I get lonesome. Who doesn't? But when I start feeling droopy and down-at-the-mouth, I clean the chicken runs or wash the down-stairs paint. There's nothing like a good job of work to cure anyone of the collywobbles. When I get done, I put my feet in the oven and pull my skirt up higher over my knees than would be decent with a man in the house, and count my blessings. I'm self-supporting and self-respecting, and beholden to no one. Any time, day or night, I can do just exactly what I feel like doing. I look over all the married women I know, and pretty soon I stop feeling sorry for myself and start thanking my lucky stars that a sense of duty prevented me from getting married. And you can take that smug look off your face, and stop laughing up your sleeve at me and thinking 'Sour Grapes,' Larry Parsons, because I mean what I say. How many eggs do you want this trip?"

Larry loaded the eggs, and we drove off. "She's a great Rienza," he said. "I think she's a little bit cracked."

I told him that if she were, I hoped I'd go crazy the same way as soon as possible. It seemed a sensible sort of lunacy to me to take the fabric of one's existence, no matter how unpromising material it seemed to be, and build as good a life of it as Rienza Trimback had done. Looking at her, I could agree with her that there are worse things than having to stand on your own two feet.

8

No Position

ONE DAY LAST spring when I was up at Middle Dam negotiating the loan of a quart of No. 30 motor oil for my rather down-at-heels Model A pick-up, I encountered John Lavorgna for the first time this season. It was the kind of day we often get in Maine in May. A gentle rain, hardly more than a drizzle, was falling steadily, and while the Carry was a little soupy in spots, the maples and birches along the way were beginning to put out their first misty red and green leaves, and the huge purple violets were blossoming in the grass between the ruts. In the swampy places the leafless rhodora blazed magenta and the shag-bush shook out a silver cloud. The mellow oboe-like notes of the white-throated sparrows' rainy-day song drifted through the hush of the dripping woods, and everything smelled of greenery and growth and the awakening earth. It was a lovely day in its own subdued fashion, and I was feeling fine as I came into the hotel lobby, shaking the water off my slicker and stamping the mud off my boots. When I saw John, sitting in the corner between two windows overlooking the lake and playing cribbage with a strange man, the day looked even better than ever to me, as it always does to all of us when we unexpectedly run across an old friend.

"John!" I cried delightedly. "When did you come In? How long are you going to stay?"

He laid his cards face down on the table, rose, and came over to shake my hand. "Came In on last night's boat. We was plannin' on stayin' a week, but unless the weather clears up so we can get some fishin'—"

I looked at him. Get some fishing indeed! It was a good day to fish, as well he should know, since he'd taught me most of what I know about fly-fishing. I started to ask him if he'd gone crazy, but something distraught in his expression stopped me. It occurred to me then that his heartiness had been slightly feverish, and I made a rapid diagnosis. He was having sports trouble.

So instead of inquiring for his wife, as I naturally would have done next, I improvised rapidly. "Oh, the barometer's started to rise. I'm going fishing myself this afternoon. They'll take anything on a rising barometer, especially at this time of year," and left him to employ that nonsense as best he could to his own advantage. We both knew that the state of the barometer has little, if anything, to do with the state of the fishing, learned opinion to the contrary, and that either the fish are rising or they aren't, depending entirely upon fish psychology, which passeth human understanding. But I did appreciate the seriousness of his position. There is nothing worse in a guide's life than a disgruntled sport, who must be babied along and kidded into thinking he's having a good time. If John could only pry his sport loose from the fireside and get him out into the nice fresh air, where he could whip the river to a lather and start the blood circulating through his veins, maybe he'd feel enough better to decide not to go home on the next train after all. But it had to be managed tactfully and there was nothing more I could do to further the campaign. So I left the warmth of the open fire and went over to where Al Parsons was sorting and labeling merchandise in her haven behind the counter.

She looked up at me and shook her head slowly, her beautiful and expressive eyes lively with suppressed laughter. "Poor John," she murmured. "His sport's getting him down. I've been sitting here all morning listening to him put on his Maine guide act. He's an artist." She raised her voice. "Since you're going fishing this afternoon, Louise, you really ought to stock up on these Carrie Stevens Gray Ghosts. They're killers. Only seventy-five cents, too. I'm sorry I can't go with you, but Larry's Outside on business and I can't leave the office."

"That'll be the Day," I told her, unimpressed. Al is about as much interested in fishing as I am in feather-stitching. "Besides, I'm not going fishing. I just said that. I'm really going to clean my kitchen cupboards and maybe wash a little paint in the living room. As you undoubtedly suspected."

She wrote the price neatly on a box of Montreals. "You and John. The great Maine nature writer and the great Maine guide. Listen to him now."

John's voice, vibrant with sincerity and conviction, rose above the snapping of the fire and the drumming of rain on the roof. "—believe there's a lot in it. I rec'lect one time up on the Allegash—just such a day as this it was, too—we started in fishin' right after lunch on a risin' barometer, an' I never saw the beat of it—"

"Well, this isn't getting any potatoes sprouted," I told

Al. "What I came up for was to see if I could borrow some motor oil."

"Sure. Swene's up in the engine house. Ask him about it."

My oil deal completed, I went back into the office to say good-bye to Al, but she was busy selling some Gray Ghosts to John's sport, so that they could take advantage of the wholly mythical rise of the barometer to go fishing after lunch. She winked at me over the bowed head of her customer and then turned the bland and innocent eye of an old con man on him. There was nothing to be gained by hanging around, so I started the Ford and went home, laughing to myself and thinking that what John had once said to me about a guide's job was certainly true.

"Wal, it ain't no position," he'd said. "It sure ain't no position!"

I've known John for seventeen years, ever since I first came to Maine as a schoolteacher-on-vacation. He was the first Maine guide I'd ever laid eyes on, and I still consider him the best, after having known more guides than you could shake a stick at. The first thing about John to impress me was that he looked like a guide, or at least like my idea at the time of how a guide should look. Since then I've discovered that a guide can look like practically anything from a Judge of the Supreme Court to a housewife. I'm a licensed guide myself, now, so I ought to know. In those days, however, my notions about Maine were derived entirely from reading. John was dark, with the Indian cast to his features which all the books had led me to expect—his profile would look very well on a coin; and he dressed properly, too, in soft, soleless moccasins, faded plaid shirts, and a battered old felt hat with salmon flies stuck carelessly into the crown.

I met him during the month of August, when the fishing isn't very good and the guides, instead of taking out fisher-men, which is comparatively easy, have to choose between loafing or conducting what amounts to sight-seeing tours of the country. That's hard work. Fishermen may be mono-maniacs, but their peculiar obsession at least keeps them amused and tied down to one spot and one easily answered set of questions, like "Do you think I'd better change to a Royal Coachman?" The August canoe-trippers want to cover territory, experience in four days everything the woods have to offer, and learn every single last bit of available data on anything they see or hear about. I know all about that, too, because during the first phase of my acquaintanceship with John, I was a sight-seeing sport myself, with all the attitudes that I have since come to deplore in others. That's how I met John. He guided four or five of us starry-eyed and palpitating nature lovers up to Little Boy Falls, above Parmachene, near the Canadian border.

We thought he was simply wonderful. One of the more romantic-minded and effusive young women of the party said he was an unspoiled son of the wilderness, living in tune with the earth and the elements. She said she couldn't imagine his ever being tamed and shackled by civilization and con-vention. She said he was brother of all that was wild and free and natural, one with wind and wave. She really did say all those things, and the funny part of it is that the rest of us, men and women alike, secretly agreed with her, even though we did think it sounded a little bit silly spoken out loud. It was obvious that John did love the woods and lakes. He apparently found the spectacle of an old vixen playing with her cubs on a sunny ledge overlooking Cupsuptic just as appealing and entertaining as the rest of us did, although to him it was a commonplace. His accustomed eyes saw a thousand things that escaped ours—twin, coin-spotted fawns standing motionless in the shade of a tree, blending perfectly with the sun-shot shadow; two tiny song-birds darting and crying in a frenzy about the head of a great hawk, driving it in ignominious retreat from the neighborhood of their nest; an enormous bald eagle perched majestically on the tip of a dead pumpkin pine. To us these things were strange and new, so it isn't surprising that we found them marvelous. It is surprising that he too found them something to marvel at, for all their familiarity. Nobody who didn't truly love the wilderness could have counterfeited the pure delight John took in everything about it, from the fall of light across a far mountain range to the anxious industry of the ants among the crumbs about our feet as we ate lunch on a lake shore. Nobody who didn't love the wilderness to his very bones would have put up with us as the price for the privilege of moving along the high valleys, as most people move through the rooms of their houses. John could have had a nice peaceful life working in a mill, after all.

I don't think we were any worse than most of the August parties, but I'm very sure John didn't return the compliment by thinking we were wonderful. We were, I'm sure, indistinguishable from the scores of other safaris that he's conducted through the same country from year to year. We wore the same unsuitable clothes—shorts in black-fly season and pleated slacks in brush terrain. We had the same dietary peculiarities—the man with ulcers who couldn't eat fried food and the woman who had to have Sanka. We had the gentleman with the sacroiliac which precluded him from helping with the hard work, and the camera fiend who periodically put a spoke in the wheels of progress by making us freeze in our tracks, usually when John had a heavy work canoe on his shoulders, while he took pictures. We got tired and too hot or too cold, and some of us complained. All of us expected the guide to be either ignorant of or indifferent to the concept of an eight-hour working day. Just because he'd served breakfast at six A.M. didn't seem to us to be any logical reason why he shouldn't take us fishing until dark, even if it did mean he was doing dishes and making up bough beds at ten forty-five P.M. And we asked the same old questions, inevitably, that John had answered a thousand times before and knew he was going to answer a couple of thousand times to come. We certainly were no treat to him; but I guess he was wonderful at that, because he never let us suspect the truth. He gave us a good time, and if it was with the ease of long practice that he did so, we were never aware of it.

Let me give you a sample day in John's life. It doesn't make much difference what day or who is taking the current trip, because the days and the sports vary very little. It is John's first responsibility to get his party out and back without allowing anyone to come to greater grief than a few black-fly bites, minor cuts and abrasions, and medium-painful sunburns. But the fundamental safety precautions have become automatic with him, so that his chief conscious concern is to keep his sports happy, contented, and reasonably comfortable.

To this end, he arises between half past four and five in the morning, builds a fire, and starts the coffee. Long ago he discovered that there are people in the world whom it is as much as your life is worth to speak to or even look at until after they have had their coffee, and that this condition is aggravated by their having spent a restless night under unaccustomed sleeping conditions. When John makes coffee, he makes coffee, what I mean. He puts a pound of grounds into a gallon pot, breaks in an egg, throws the shell and some salt in after it, and stirs it up into a nauseating-looking mess. Then he fills the pot with cold water and sets it on to boil. When it has boiled up once, he sets it back to keep hot and settle, pouring a little cold water down the spout to hasten the process. It comes out strong as lye and clear as crystal. It's wonderful. Once when I complimented him on it, he said he didn't believe in no shadow coffee. He liked his drinks to have some authority. "Take Scotch now," he said. "If the Lord intended there should be water in it, He'd have put it in in the first place. I don't drink much, but when I do, I don't do no tamperin' with Divine Will."

I asked him what shadow coffee was. "Why, you know," he said. "It's when a feller sets a pan of water on the fire and hangs a bag of coffee over it. When the shadow of the bag has crossed the water, he calls the coffee done." I did indeed know what he meant.

Then John eats his own breakfast, because after his sports get up, he won't have time. The Maine guide's idea of breakfast is Something: oranges, bacon or ham and eggs, fried potatoes, toast and griddle cakes with maple syrup, doughnuts and a lot of coffee. All the sports who say, "But I *never* have anything except fruit juice and coffee for breakfast!" end by eating everything. Then the dishes have to be washed, and because the hot water supply is limited, they are first rinsed in the lake and scoured with sand. Then they can be scalded, dried, and packed. Next the blankets have to be shaken out and rolled and put into the canoes, and the camp waste has to be burned. At last everything is done, and John takes a last survey of the camp-site, because too often in his career he has had to turn back after two hours of paddling into a head wind to retrieve a camera someone has left hanging on a bush, or a bottle of vitamin pills someone else cached in a tree crotch for safe and handy keeping. On these final reconnoiterings he always collects a sweater or two, a pair of moccasins, and a few bath towels. Then the fire is doused with a pail of water, and all is ready for the shove-off.

The morning is spent in paddling to the lunch ground, probably six miles away, and this isn't as easy on the guide as it sounds. If the fleet consists of more than two canoes, he has to try to keep within easy reach of all of them, in case of accident. Very few sports know much about paddling—oh, they can shove a keeled canoe around Norumbega Park, all right, but the keelless work canoes of the woods are something else again, and the sustained effort required to cover fifteen miles a day of open lake is not quite like dallying around a duck pond—and they have a tendency to lag and scatter. The guide needs eyes in the back of his head to keep them all under supervision. Furthermore, he has, for safety's sake, taken the least proficient member of the party for his own bowman, and there are times when he concludes that he could do better alone, paddling a dishpan with a slotted mixing spoon. He may be just sitting still in a canoe, but he's pretty busy all the same.

The noon meal is the simplest of the day, in the interests of making time. It usually consists of a chowder or stew, topped off with fruit and cookies. John encourages his sports to go swimming while he's preparing lunch. It's something to keep them amused and out from under foot. In spite of good intentions and great zeal, they sometimes hinder more than they help. So John tells them to swim and get cool and rested, and afterwards, if they want to, they can help clean up. It works out very well, and an hour later the expedition is afloat again, with eight or ten miles to cover before pulling out for the night.

The afternoon is like the morning, only harder on the guide, because his sports are now tired and more inclined than ever to loaf and straggle. If this routine of just pushing a canoe around all day sounds a little dull, let me assure you that it isn't. The country is so beautiful, so ever-changing, that boredom is impossible. Then there is always the fascination—to me at least—of entering new country under my own power, country that is inaccessible to the sissies that depend on railroad trains and hard-surfaced roads. New vistas are opened with every promontory that is rounded, and the light changes continually on the mountains. The other traffic on the lake provides matter for speculation. Where in the world did that woman in a Mother Hubbard and a flowered hat come from and where does she think she's going in that leaky old rowboat? Or why are those two men just sitting and drifting in the middle of the lake, miles from shore, talking to each other so earnestly and seriously? Maybe they're plotting murder and chose this place as being eaves-dropper-proof. It's fun to think so, anyhow. There's a point with a dead pine on it. It must be the one John was telling about at lunch, where the three men were drowned last year, just off shore. Oh, there's plenty to keep one entertained on a canoe trip.

At about half past five, while the sun is still high, the night's camp site is reached. Dinner won't be until seven or so, so this is the recreation period. That is, for everyone except John. Others can go swimming or fishing, or lie on the grass swapping stories or just smoking and relaxing, or write in their diaries, or change into clean clothes and wash their others, or prowl around with bird books in their hands, snooping on the private lives of hermit thrushes, or collect botanical specimens, or read pocket mysteries, or make daisy chains, for that matter; but not John. He has to prepare dinner. He peels the potatoes and vegetables and sets them on to boil, gets the steaks salted and ready for last-minute broiling, starts the coffee, opens cans of peaches and finds the boxed chocolate cake for dessert, and decides he has time to make hot bis-cuits. Since he has no oven, this is accomplished in a heavy, covered, iron spider—or frying pan, if you prefer—balanced on two stones near the flame, but not too near, and turned occasionally to insure even baking. It's quite a trick, much harder than, but nowhere near as spectacular as, turning pancakes by flipping them.

I happened on John once while he was mixing his biscuit dough, and I was shocked and disillusioned to find that he was using a prepared commercial mix, simply adding water as the directions said. "Why, John," I said, more in sorrow than in anger, "I'm disappointed. I thought only greenhorns used that stuff."

His composure was unruffled. "Heed what I say," he told me. "It's the greenhorns that make work for themselves, totin' lard an' flour an' bakin' powder 'round all day an' spendin' half the evenin' mixin' them up. You see a feller doin' it the easy way, you'll know you're lookin' at an old hand. There's enough trouble connected with guidin' that can't be helped without lookin' for more." I've remembered this, and I've found it to be true. The experienced old woodsmen have no false pride about being caught with modern conveniences in their duffle. The only reason they don't pack electric blankets is that they can't plug them into a tree.

After dinner is over and the dishes done, John has to cut boughs and make bough beds. This is not a matter of just throwing down a few branches in a heap, but of laying the small feathery twigs in courses, like shingles, with the tips curled up. Then he has to dole out the blankets, because there's always someone whose mother was frightened by a snowdrift or something, so he thinks he's entitled to more blankets than normal people. After this, if John is lucky, nobody happens to think how much fun it would be to go paddling by moonlight or jacking deer with a flashlight. If he's unlucky in these respects, he doesn't get his party to bed until midnight. Then he goes around picking up all the shoes that are lying on the ground in spite of his warning about porcupines' dietary habits and hanging them on bushes. He takes one last look around camp, rakes the fire into a compact heart so that there will be a bed of coals in the morning, and turns in. During the average night he is aroused three times to explain that the crackling and blowing and snorting in the bushes is only a deer, startled by the smell of smoke; that nobody is yelling for help out on the lake, it's just a loon; and that porcupines neither bite nor throw quills. Just as everyone seems finally to have settled down, it's five o'clock and time to start the breakfast coffee.

I've forgotten a great many things about that first trip with John, and many of the details I have confused with the events of subsequent trips; for the first one was so successful that it led to others during the next three years. I've forgotten the names and the faces of most of the other people who went, for example, and why we had to wait for two hours once at Aziscoos Dam, and how it happened that we were sitting in a row one day on the tumbled-down wall of an ancient, lost, and forgotten cemetery, smoking and talking. But some things I'll never forget.

I'll never forget the riddle John asked us that day at Aziscoos, to keep us amused after we'd exhausted the possibilities of the water front, skipped flat stones across the lake until our arms were lame, and played stick-knife for half an hour. Some delays on trips are inevitable, and then it's up to the guide to keep his sports from becoming restive as best he can. John said suddenly, "There was a feller out on a huntin' trip. He left his camp early in the mornin' an' walked three miles due south. He see a bear there, an' shot it an' dressed it out. Then he walked three miles due west, without seein' no game. He was gettin' hungry by this time, so he turned north an' walked three miles till he come to his camp, where he cooked lunch. What color was the bear?"

"What do you mean, what color was the bear?" we demanded. "You can't tell what color was the bear from the facts you've given."

"Yes, you can, too," John stated positively.

"Say it again. Say it slow this time." So he said it again, slow, and we still didn't know what color the bear was.

"It was white," John announced confidently, and we all asked indignantly how he got that way. He must have left something out of the story. "No, I didn't neither leave nothin' out of the story," he said. "Look. He went south, he went west, he went north." He drew an isosceles triangle on the sun-bleached boards of the landing with the point of his sheath knife, and labeled them respectively S, W, and N. "There's only one place in the world you can do that an' come back to where you started, an' that's right at the North Pole. So the bear must have been white, because the only kind of bear lives up there is a polar bear."

I don't know where John picked that up, but it served its purpose. By the time we'd got it through our thick heads, and then memorized it for use against the unwary, the boat that was supposed to pick us up came along, and the situation was saved.

The day we were sitting on the cemetery wall, he remarked that he took an interest in cemeteries because he used to have charge of one, over near Paris. We took this in our stride, since Maine is full of names like Paris and Norway and Calais—only that's pronounced Careless, here—and China. "Paris, France, I mean," John added as an afterthought.

"Paris, *France?* What were you doing in a cemetery there?"

"Oh, it was right after the last war, an' there was this big American military cemetery near Paris. It come under the Army's say-so, an' they happened to put a bunch from my outfit to work in it. I was straw-boss, as you might say. It was real nice work. I enjoyed it. That was how I come to make the acquaintance of President Wilson."

"You mean Woodrow Wilson?"

"Yup. Seems he was over there tendin' out on some kind of a Peace Conference. Wal, one mornin' early I was out in the cemetery, an' I see this feller walkin' around among the graves. It was real pretty out there that mornin'—dew all over the grass an' the flowers bright an' fresh. I thought prob'ly he was lookin' for some special grave—someone that belonged to him, maybe—so I went up an' asked him if I could help him. Course I didn't realize who he was, though he did look a little familiar, or I wouldn't have bothered him. He said no, he doubted I could help him. He needed some help, but it warn't the kind no one else could give him, so he'd come out there alone to sort of mull things over and get them straight in his mind. He said it was a good place to think, quiet, with all the boys lyin' there, bringin' to mind things best not forgot. Then it come to me who he was, an' I started away, but he wouldn't have it. He wanted to know what we were plannin' on doin' in the cemetery; he seemed interested and had some good suggestions to give. He was real nice-spoken, an' we had a good talk. He seemed sort of a sad man, an' I liked him an' felt sorry for him both at the same time, that mornin' in the cemetery near Paris, France."

I'll never forget the first and fundamental rules of fishing that John taught me. We were up at Little Boy, camped there for three days just below the lovely little falls, and he was employing a free half-hour before supper to catch a mess of pan trout in the pool. Most of the party were stretched out on the blanket-rolls, resting, or washing out socks in the river.

"Hey," I said, watching him cast. "Let me try that. It looks easy as pie." I made two mistakes in those few words. The first one I discovered almost at once: it was not easy as pie. The second I didn't recognize until a long time later, because John was too polite to point it out to me, and besides, the guide is supposed to take a beating. That's what he's hired for. I should never have expected him to let me use his rod. Devout fishermen will give away anything they own, sooner than loan their pet rod for even a few minutes. I feel the same way about my own now, and I'd cut my tongue out rather than ask to borrow anyone else's. But I didn't know any better then.

"I'll teach you how to cast," said John, reeling in, "if you'll promise me three things. I don't aim to set loose on the world none of these here uneducated fishermen. There's enough of them foulin' up the works already. If you're hell-bent to fish, you're goin' to fish like a gentleman. The first rule: Don't *never* ask a feller what kind of a fly or lure he's usin'. Sets you down as ignorant right off the bat. Second: Don't *never* lay your line down across another feller's nor fish close enough to him to crowd him. An' third: Don't ever kill no more fish than you're plannin' on usin'. That's bein' a fish-hog. That's about all the important rules, an' if you stick by 'em, you'll come out all right."

I promised, and I've stuck by it, and so far at least I guess I've come out all right.

It seems incredible to me now that I once had to be taught how to pronounce the names of the places which are to-day practically extensions of my own backyard, names which I use as commonly as a New Yorker uses Madison or Broadway. But it's true, and John was the one who corrected me kindly—me and about a thousand others like me—when I said "*Um*bagog." It's Um-*bay*-gog. He taught me that Aziscoos has four syllables, Az-iss-coe-hoss, and that the Dead Cambridge and the Dead Diamond aren't called that because corpses were found on their banks, but only to distinguish them from the Swift Cambridge and the Swift Diamond, rivers with rapids in them where the dead rivers have none. With endless patience he explained, probably for about the seven-hundredth time, that only city slickers say "venison."

Natives call it deer-meat, unless they've been living on it all winter, when they're apt to refer to it as old goat. That was a lesson I've found very valuable since I've set up shop as a native myself.

I remember one day when John had been dragooned into guiding a party on a mountain-climbing trip, although I can't remember what possible contingency had involved me in any such project, since I regard mountain climbing with loathing. All that work for what? A view. I know where there are plenty of views that I can enjoy without having to half-kill myself to get to them. We were resting—probably at my insistence—beside a little pond part way up the darned mountain, when John pointed to what looked to me like a heap of sticks and brush, but which was actually a beaver house. Naturally we were all fascinated, and John was interested, too, but for a different reason.

"Crimus," he said, "there's a lot of beaver in there. I'd ought to put in some beaver sets here this winter—only this year I've swore off trappin' beaver."

We'd heard about swearing off a lot of things, but never beaver trapping, so we wanted to know why.

"Wal, I'll tell you how 'tis. I was down to Boston to the Sportsman's Show last winter, workin' on the State of Maine exhibit. Never put in such a turrible ten days in my life, not even countin' the second time I had pneumonia. It sure was fierce. They'll never get me down there again."

"Why? What was the matter with it?"

"Everything was the matter with it," he stated sweepingly. "Place was crowded with a million people all tryin' to think up a sillier question to ask than the next feller. An' I couldn't stand all them critters in cages. I shoot an' trap animals, but

I don't hold with torturin' them, shuttin' them up for people to gawk at, an' poke at, an' scare half to death. That ain't right. An' when you went outside the buildin', it was as much as your life was worth. Cars goin' every-which-way, sixty miles a minute. I sure was glad when I got back to God's country. Only one good thing happened all the time I was there.

"Like I say I was workin' on the State of Maine exhibit. We had a good exhibit, too, if I do say it as shouldn't. We'd brought down a mess of live beaver, an' we built a place for them. We had a brook fallin' down over some rocks into a little pool-like, an' all around the edge we stuck up some little trees, like they was growin'. Looked real natural. You couldn't see the wire fence on account of the trees, an' we hid the drain the water ran out of with some bushes an' tall grass. Best exhibit in the show—though New Hampshire was pretty good, too. They had a moose an' an albino porcupine. Last thing the night before the show opened, we put the beaver in the pool an' left them to make theirselves to home."

He laughed, his teeth white in his dark face, his eyes narrowed and bright. "They sure made themselves to home all right. When we come in next mornin', the whole place was flooded, with water runnin' out under the doors. Them little devils had gnawed down half the trees an' dammed up the drain. By golly, they must have flew right at it, to get all that work done in one night. Took all hands till noon to get the place cleaned an' dried up enough to open the show. I sure had to laugh, though there were some who didn't think it was very comical. We had to post a guard every night after that, to discourage them."

He threw his cigarette end into the water and stood up in one flowing motion. "Then 'twas that I decided to lay off beaver trappin' this winter. It seemed kind of ungrateful to kill the little cusses after they give me the only laugh I got out of the whole ten days of the show."

The next year we took a trip up into this country, I met and married Ralph, and my days as a sport were over. I became one of the few to pass over and stand on the other side of the great gulf that is fixed between the native and the sport minds, and my relationship with John changed completely. Then it was that I discovered to my surprise that he leads a double life. Heretofore I had seen him only in his professional capacity, as the type of *coureur de bois*, dashing, gay, glamorous. Now I found out about the other aspect of his life.

When John was about twenty or so, he had occasion to spend some time up around Jackman. Two people seem to have made an impression on him during that period. The first was Mary Pickford, who was spending the summer at a camp on Moosehead. When I asked him what she looked like in the flesh, he said that she had pretty hair, adding, "She'd ought to have. She combed it enough. All she done was comb her hair. Every time I went past the place, there she was settin' out by the lake, combin' an' combin' an' combin'." The other person was Mabel, and I wouldn't be surprised at all if Mabel, at sixteen, had just as pretty hair as Mary Pickford. It's still pretty, short and dark and curly, around a high-cheekboned little face with big dark eyes gazing out of it. At sixteen she must have been cute as a button. John thought she was, anyhow, and apparently he wasn't the only one. He had plenty of rivals when he started to tend out on her, as we say here. He did the usual—bought her candy, took her canoeing, and escorted her to dances. I'll bet he was no slouch for looks himself in those days; and pretty soon they had arrived at what I believe is called "an understanding." This is not quite as serious as a formal betrothal, but in this country it's considered fairly binding, just the same.

Then one night she went to a dance with someone else. I don't blame her at all. She was quite within her rights, and there is nothing more infuriating than being taken for granted. But John didn't adopt my broader view. He thought it was terrible. If she was going to be his girl, she was going to *be* his girl, and no two ways about it. He laid it down to her that he wouldn't stand for any of this shilly-shallying around, and the upshot was that they eloped and were married that very day. AND have lived happily ever after.

John and Mabel started out as most young people in this country do, without much money, but with a great willingness to work, an understanding of what hard work is, and a good idea of what they wanted. They wanted a nice home, a good life together, and a large enough savings account to see them safely through their old age. They bought an old house in a state of disrepair, and set about fixing it up. John could do much of the carpentry himself, and Mabel could paint and hang paper, so the project shouldn't cost too much. But it was rather slow work at that, because during the summer Mabel worked as a cabin girl at a near-by camp, and of course John was away guiding much of the time. Out of their earnings they gradually replaced the things they'd set up housekeeping with, by buying a piece at a time, preferring to make-do with what they had until they could afford what they wanted. They installed a bathroom and a modern kitchen, and planted little fruit trees alongside the house. John reclaimed the big garden that had gone back to grass and put in every vegetable that can be grown in this climate and some that people said couldn't; and Mabel spent many of her summer evenings, when she was through at the camp for the day, and more long autumn days, canning and preserving.

I was down in her cellar once, and I never saw such a sight. The walls were lined from floor to ceiling with shelves crammed with jars, each labeled with the contents and the date. There were glowing red beets, scarlet tomatoes, and little golden carrots no bigger than your finger. There were pints of dark dandelion greens, which she'd dug in field and meadow when they were still young and tender in the early spring, and of lighter green Swiss chard, and slender string beans and young peas. There were rows and rows of blueberries and wild raspberries and cranberries, which you can have for the picking in this country, and smooth peach halves, and pale spiced pears in syrup. There was shelf after shelf of relishes, and picallili, and chutney, and jewel-toned jellies, and all kinds of pickles—mustard, dill, bread-and-butter, gherkin, and plain sweet and sour. Then there was an entire section given over to game—whole little partridges in jellied stock, rabbit meat that looked like chicken, deer steaks which had been browned lightly and rolled before being packed in glass, rich deer-meat stew, and jars of mincemeat, made from the necks and scraps of the deer. Some of the labels said "John's Deer" and some said "Mabel's Deer," with the year, because they both hunted during the season, and

Mabel was a better shot than John, although she wouldn't admit it.

I once saw her make an impossible long shot at a rabbit, shooting quickly from an off-balance position as it ran across an opening in the trees. When it rolled over and over and then lay still, we all stood in stunned and incredulous silence for a moment before bursting into cheers. "Luck," said Mabel. "You ought to see John—" Well, I've seen John shoot, and he's good. But I've seen Mabel make shots like that more than once, and she's better. John says so, too. He brags about it. The day I was in Mabel's cellar, I turned from the rows of sparkling glass and said, "Good Lord, Mabel, I hate to think of all the hours and hours of work that went into this." And I did, too. I don't mind picking berries or beans and pulling carrots or beets, although you can get an awful crick in your back doing either; but if there's anything I hate, it's stewing over a hot stove, sterilizing jars and testing seals, when the day outdoors is blue and gold and everyone else has gone swimming. Things always arrive at the perfect canning stage just when the weather is best outside, for some perverse reason. "Anyway," I comforted both of us, "you won't go hungry this winter."

"No, we don't aim to. When John gets the potatoes and root-crops dug, and the cabbages and squashes in, and the apples picked, we'll be pretty well fixed for everything except coffee and sugar and flour. You never have to go hungry in the country, if you're willing to work." She led the way upstairs. "I'm planning to make a big braided rug for the living room this winter. I've been saving material for a year. And John's going to build me some bookshelves and another kitchen cupboard to keep my new aluminum in. We're finally getting pretty well straightened out. Like everybody, we've had some set-backs—sickness to be paid for and the pipes freezing and bursting winter before last—so it's taken a long time. But it looks now like we're in the clear at last."

And the next thing I knew, the house had burned flat, one evening when they were out for a short time. They didn't save a thing. All that they had worked so hard for over a period of more than a quarter of a century was reduced to a heap of smoking rubble and broken Mason jars in the bottom of an open cellar hole. Even the fruit trees were charred and killed by the heat.

I saw John shortly after that, and he was a little discouraged, but not unduly so. "Folks have been awful good to us," he said. "Those Wilmots that I've guided sent us a pair of wonderful Hudson Bay blankets, and the Grabeys sent a half a dozen sheets and pillow cases. And folks around town— Why, you wouldn't believe it! They turned out their attics and give us everything they could spare. Course, the chairs don't all match—but we can set on them just the same. Some of the pots and pans are a little dented, but they'll hold water. Like I said to Mabel, they're better'n what we started out with, an' what we done once, we can do again. Chief thing I feel bad about—Mabel had just bought herself a new dress. She put an awful store by it. Liked it best of any dress she ever had. She was savin' it to wear somewhere special—an' now of course she never will get to put it on."

"That is too bad," I said. "What are you going to do now, John? Rebuild?"

"Nope. I'm buyin' another house—that one next to the schoolhouse, down home. It's in turrible shape, but when we get done with it— You know, you learn a lot, fixin' up a house.

We made plenty of mistakes on the old one. Things look like they'd work out fine sometimes, but they don't when you come to live with them. There's a lot of mistakes we won't make again. Course, this has set us back some. Guess I won't be retirin' now, when I get to be sixty, like I always said I was goin' to. But I dunno what I'd do with myself anyhow, settin' around all day suckin' my thumb. An' this way, when we get done we'll have a home worth ownin'.'"

Since then I've been through the town where he lives several times. It's only a little town, and you can see practically all of it as you sit in the lone day coach, which with a baggage car, makes up the train. You have a very good view of John's house, across some fields and a shady road. At first it looked pretty shabby and bare, but it wasn't long before I noticed new shingles on the roof and the start of a new paint job. A year or so later, the chimneys had been repointed and I could see flower beds blazing bright beside the front door and a big vegetable garden laid out in the side lot. The whole place was beginning to look well-cared-for and prosperous, with the windows gleaming and white curtains crisp behind them. The last time I went through, there was a big porch under construction; so I concluded, safely I think, that the important inside remodeling had been completed, and that John and Mabel were well on their way to seeing their goal achieved.

It was at about that time that I developed my theory concerning John. Like most of my theories, it embraces a little fact and a lot of assumption, so it shouldn't be taken too seriously. The fact is that John is part Indian, part Italian, and part Yankee. According to my theory, his Indian blood accounts for his love of and skill in the woods, his Italian blood accounts for his poise and fluency and social grace, and his

Yankee blood accounts for his dependability, industry, and integrity. Since we all have known woods-stupid Indians, surly Italians, and no-good Yankees, this theory obviously won't bear too close inspection; but, though a poor thing, it is mine own, and I like it.

I saw John last only a few days ago. I'd driven up to Middle for the mail, but when I arrived there, the boat wasn't in. In fact, it hadn't even started for South Arm, because it had to go to Upper Dam first to pick up John and a party he was guiding. I looked around for Al Parsons, but she was in conference with the chef, and after that she had to type the dinner menus. I have very strong principles against bothering people when they are trying to do their work. One of the very hardest things about living in any resort country is finding time to attend to your own business. Everyone is in a carefree vacation mood, with no responsibilities, and they don't see any reason why you can't enter into the spirit of play. So I wandered down to the dock, and when the boat came in from Upper Dam, got aboard with the idea of going down to the Arm just for the ride. John was aboard with his sports, and greeted me with a casual nod, not missing a syllable of what he was saying to a gentleman who looked as though he might have a bad sacroiliac as well as a predilection for Sanka. I winked at John and went forward to discuss with Swene Meisener, the boatman, the case of my ailing Reo truck. My principles against bothering men at work extend to John.

I could hear his voice running on behind me as I outlined the Reo's symptoms to Swene, and just as we had decided that there was probably a pinhole in the carbureter float, I heard John say composedly, "It's called Metallic Island because it's full of mineral deposits. It's practically a solid junk of metal. An' I'll tell you another thing: It's a good place to stay 'way from in a thunderstorm. If lightenin's goin' to strike anywhere, that's the first place it heads for." There were impressed murmurs from his audience, and Swene and I exchanged guarded grins. We both knew that the island in question had about as much metal on it as you'd find in a newborn rabbit's ear, and that it was in fact not named Metallic at all, but Metalluc, after an Indian who used to live there.

In a few minutes John came forward to join us, and I muttered under my breath, "You ought to be ashamed of yourself, John Lavorgna. All that eye-wash about Metalluc."

"Sure, I suppose so," he said a little wearily. "But my God, Louise, you get sick of the same old questions and the same old answers. You like a change once in a while. They don't care what you tell them, just so long's you tell them somethin'. There's only one wrong answer a guide can give. Just so long's you don't say, '*I don't know*,' you're doin' all right. But the minute you admit you don't know, you're a gone gosling."

I said I could see what he meant. "Have you got your new porch done yet?" I changed the subject.

"Yup. Looks good, too." He glanced at his watch. "We're makin' pretty good time to-day. I'm hopin' to get home in time to put a coat of paint on it, an' maybe do some work in my garden before dark. The weeds are catchin' up with me somethin' fierce this weather, an' I don't like to have Mabel workin' out there in the hot sun. 'Tain't a woman's place."

"Did you have a good trip this time?" I inquired.

" 'Bout the same as usual." His face lighted up. "We did see one thing worth a long day's voyage. Fawn triplets. I've seen plenty of twins, but this is the first time I ever see triplets. It was a real pretty sight. Wal—I gotta get back to the salt mines." He went aft, and in a minute I heard him saying, "Look at the loon! No, right over there. Whoops, there he goes. Now watch yonder, in line with that cedar stump. That's where he'll come up. You see, loons always come up in the direction they was facin' when they dived. They can't turn around under water. See? There he is."

"Isn't he wonderful?" a feminine voice breathed; and I thought, You can say that again, Lady. Because she only knew the half of it. She had no suspicion that the John who knew loons couldn't turn around under water was only a façade for John, the solid citizen who worked in his garden until dark and got up at dawn to paint his new porch. You had to know both Johns really to appreciate him.

9

The Old She-Coon

In what my children call "the olden days," which may mean a time not more than eight years gone, lumbering was a very different proposition than it is now in this country. Those were the days of the bigger jobbers, the men who undertook on their own responsibility and cognizance to log off for the company a tract of company-owned timberland at a set price per cord for wood landed. They supplied their own equipment, met their own pay-rolls, built and ran their own camps, and used their own methods. A jobber's success depended on the soundness of his judgment, based on experience and the reports of his cruisers, when he put in his bid to the company. If he made no great error in estimating the amount of pulpwood available in a given area, or in the operating cost of his camp, or in the expense of hauling to the landing, the probability was that he would make a lot of money.

A cruiser's report can be taken at face value. If he says, after walking through the woods and observing the size and density of the blackgrowth, that the area in question will yield fifty thousand cords, you can safely assume that it will yield just about fifty thousand cords; because the cruiser is an expert, and his continuance in his job rests upon his infallibility. Any experienced jobber does not make mistakes about operating costs. He has the figures at his fingertips. He does not make mistakes either about the hauling, although it was the hauling that most often licked a jobber, for reasons that I'll explain shortly.

The contract with the company always specified that the wood would be paid for after it was delivered at the landing, which in this country is always a river or lake. The teamsters dumped it on the ice, and there the jobber's responsibility ended. Along toward spring, the company crews came in and strung booms around the winter's cut, to keep it from drifting away when the ice went out; and as soon as the lakes were clear and the wood was water-borne, it was driven to the mills fifty or a hundred miles away in New Hampshire, down the Androscoggin. But it was—and is—the jobber's business to get it from where it stood in the woods to where it was to lie on the ice. Obviously a short down-hill haul is better and cheaper than a long haul over a mountain, and a good jobber knows how many cents per cord per mile he should add on to his price to the company for the landed wood. The catch —as is always the case in any enterprise in this country, be it raising a row of radishes or running a resort hotel—is the weather, one of the few things over which the individual has no control.

Here we average, year in and year out, an aggregate snowfall of one hundred and ten inches, or almost ten feet. Of course this doesn't all lie on the ground at once, but in spite of thaws and settling, in the normal year we never see bare ground between November and April, and there is at any time three or four feet of snow coverage. This is absolutely essential to the success of a lumbering operation. Wood can't be hauled on bare ground, and roads can't be built, except at prohibitive cost, without snow. A hauling road through the woods is a remarkable thing, to me at least. The terrain here is very rough, little more than a gigantic heap of enormous boulders pushed up by the ice cap and left where it lay by the recession of the great glacier, to be covered with a thin layer of leaf mold and soil. Great pits lie between the boulders and big trees thrust up among them. When the ground is bare, it's difficult even to walk through the woods, off the trails, let alone drive a team of horses and a sled through them. The snow changes all that. The boss decides where the roads are to run and sets to work a crew of daymen. First they cut down the trees that stand in the way, and then they fill the pits with brush and anything else they can lay hands on. Then when the snow comes, they shovel it in and trample it down until the road is as level as a floor and frozen as hard as concrete. Of course, when spring comes and the snow melts, the road vanishes into thin air; but it has served its purpose.

The best road I ever saw in the woods was one Roy Bragg had running the mile from Sunday Pond to Sunday Cove. He kept a crew working on it all the time, leveling the sunken spots, watering the ruts in places where the going was hard, and spreading road-hay on the slippery down-pitches, where a heavy load might overrun the horses. Road-hay has to be spread every day, because the deer come out and eat it every night, and shaken up between loads, because it gets trodden down and slick. Roy's road was so good that it inspired his teamsters to run a contest as to who could haul the largest load without sluicing his team. I sat all one afternoon with the scaler in the office, waiting for the teams to come down the valley and pause in the camp yard, so that the load could be scaled, before going along to the landing. The scaler and I were not the only ones who rushed out of the overheated little tar-paper shacks into the pinching dry cold of the clearing when we heard the jangle of harness and the shouts of the teamsters approaching. Doors slammed everywhere, and the entire stay-at-home personnel of the camp—the cook and cookees and bull-cook, the clerk and stamper and feeders—all streamed out to stand shivering while the scale was taken. The winner that afternoon brought down six and a half cords behind a team of four wiry, half-wild little bays, who showed the whites of their eyes and blew out their breaths through red-lined nostrils as they leaned into the collars and pawed for purchase with their sharp-shod hooves. Six and a half cords of green wood is a lot to haul on one load, and everyone cheered the stouthearted little team when the scale was read. It was exciting and somehow moving.

An open winter, such as we sometimes get, made it impossible for a jobber to build roads like that, and the result was likely to be that spring found him with half his cut still piled back in the woods, and the company adamant on the subject of paying for pulp as yet unlanded. This wasn't as serious as it sounds, in practice. The wood wasn't going to spoil in a year, and it wasn't eating its head off. The jobber could go back the next year and haul it out, and in the meantime it served as collateral if he had to borrow money, as he usually did. Things were different in those olden days of twenty years ago. It was easy to raise money, and if the jobber went into the red this year, next year he'd probably clean up twenty thousand dollars. Business was more of a gamble then, and the jobbers acted like gamblers. They tightened their belts and borrowed a stake at the end of a bad season, and at the end of a good one they rode around in Packard Straight Eights and their women wore mink. And it was in those days that Bill Greenwood—only he was Bill Boisvert then, just as Joe Field was Joe de la Pasture—married Frances, a Canadian woman with a dash of Indian blood.

Then times changed, and the jobber had greater obstacles to overcome than the vagaries of the weather. Federal regulations made the borrowing of money from the banks more difficult, and the Federal income tax devoured larger and larger slices of the good years' profits. The flow of cheap labor from across the border was cut off. You could still bring men over, but only under bond, and these bonded men—or Canadian prisoners, as they were, with fair accuracy, called—were often more bother than they were worth. They got into trouble, breaking the game laws or being drunk and disorderly, and had to be rescued from jail; and when it came time to return them to Canada, sometimes they couldn't be found. New wage and hour laws were enacted, although because lumbering comes under the same heading as agricultural and seasonal employment, this didn't affect the logging as much as it did some other industries. But it had some effect, as did the new state health regulations of camps, and the Social Security acts. The days when a jobber was absolute monarch in his own territory were over. He now had to do what one Government or another said, and it was a hard lesson to learn for men who had never taken orders from anyone. In addition to all that, the good places had been logged off, leaving only those areas where the timber was so difficult of access that it would take a very smart man to job it at a profit.

One by one the big jobbers, whose names had been synonymous with power and wealth, who were almost legends in the country, folded. Roy Bragg, who had for sentiment's sake kept on his pay-roll a roistering, bawdy crew of old lumberjacks and river-hogs past their working days, is dead and most of his bravos are on old-age pensions. Silas Huntoon, a deceptively mild and gentle-mannered man whom his woodsmen loved, broke his heart and lost his shirt on the ledges of Grafton Notch, trying to run an impossible operation among the sparse growth and icy cliff-faces of that evil place. He lives alone now in a great old house, not speaking to anyone, adrift in some world of his own. The Thurstons are gone, one crushed by a runaway sled and the other helpless in bed. A few of the others work for the company now, running the camps on wages under company auspices, little more than straw-bosses, no longer solely responsible for the success or failure of the job, no longer very much interested. It was only a matter of time, everyone said, before Bill Greenwood went the way of the rest.

But Bill Greenwood didn't fold. Instead he took a job down in South Arm, and built a big camp on a narrow bench above the lake, with the abrupt shore dropping into the deep and quiet waters almost from the office steps, and the mountain rising steep and forbidding behind the cookhouse. The whole Arm is a forbidding place in winter at best. There the mountains around the lake draw together until they pinch it off into nothing at the Pocket. You can feel them closing in on you as you come down from the open lake above, almost— or so it seems to me—like the jaws of a trap. The late-rising sun of winter never clears the east wall of the mountains until almost noon, and then marches briefly across the slit of sky to drop behind the west ridge and leave the place to a long and cheerless twilight. You can stand in the Arm at three o'clock in the afternoon and see sunlight golden on the ice two miles to the north, where the lake spreads out; but it looks like a picture of another, happier country from where you shiver in a bone-chilling gloom. The knife-edged wind howls down from the northwest, driving before it towering spectres of loose snow, keening and moaning as it comes. It's a hard-bitten, ill-visaged place, and it's the place where Frances Greenwood came to live for two winters.

I met her first in October. The Arm isn't so bad at that time of year. Some of the autumn coloring still clings to the hardwood trees, flaming against the blackgrowth on the mountain sides, and the westering sun shines on the east shore, where Larry's dock is, until quite late in the afternoon. The lake is a deep indigo laced with half-hearted whitecaps, and the sky is an azure vault. Frances could have no premonition of the rigors to come, even if she had been simply sitting, as I was, waiting for the boat to be loaded. She wasn't. She was supervising the loading of half a ton of food and a bunch of drunken woodsmen. Most crews come into the woods drunk, having fortified themselves against the great drought to come, and they often constitute a problem. They were no problem to Frances. She stood there, short and square in wool breeches, high-laced boots, and a lumberman's jacket, looking all Indian with her flat cheekbones and straight black hair, and issued curt orders, sometimes in English and sometimes in French. Larry and Swene had been standing by to lend a hand in case she needed help, but they soon went back to their own business, confident that she could handle the situation.

A bandy-legged little Frenchman with a knocked-down bucksaw frame under his arm came over to me and started telling me how pretty I was; he was well lubricated and obviously seeing things through an extremely rosy haze. Before I could gather my surprised wits, Frances was beside him, quick and light-footed as a cat. She snapped her fingers and pointed to a bench. "Shut up and sit down," she said quietly. He shut up and sat down. "I'm sorry," she apologized. "He's been drinking. They behave themselves when they're sober, but when they're drunk—" She shrugged expressively. "I'm sorry he bothered you."

"He didn't bother me any," I assured her. "After living more than ten years in the woods, it would take more than a drunken woodsman to bother me. I've seen too many of them. They're harmless."

She smiled quickly. Her teeth were very white. "Then you must be Mrs. Parsons or Mrs. Rich."

"Mrs. Rich. And you're Mrs. Greenwood." We exchanged amenities, and she went back to work. She was too busy restraining her crew from falling overboard to indulge in conversation, until the boat slacked speed and edged in close to the shore under the camp. The landing lay in the shadow of the mountain, and the water was black and still as a pool of ink, with a few red maple leaves floating on it. The air was chilly here, but there was something rather cheerful about the way the light of the kerosene lamps glowed in the windows of the buildings and a handful of men streamed down the bank to meet the boat. She got her crew safely ashore without anyone's wetting more than his feet, and turned her attention to a young man with a pencil over his ear and a clipboard on his arm, the badges of office of the clerk. They started checking the load as it was put ashore.

"Where's Bill?" he asked. "Didn't he come back with you?"

She finished a count she was making before she answered.

"A dozen cases of milk— No; he'll be In Friday." She turned to Larry. "You won't forget to pick him up Friday?"

Larry said, "Nope, I won't forget. Friday. I'll get your beef from Armours at the same time. All set? Then we've got to be getting along."

The clerk cast off the mooring lines, and she called to me over the widening strip of water, "Stop in and see me when you go past. Any time. The coffee pot is always on." I said I would, and returned the invitation.

After we were out of earshot, Larry shook his head. "Bill Greenwood has gone to the hospital for a check-up. I hope he makes it back by Friday. She probably knows what she's doing."

"She probably does," I agreed. "She looks competent to me. But what about the job? Who's in charge if Bill's away?"

Larry shrugged. "I guess she is. Seems like an awful lot for her to take on, managing that bunch of halligans. Running a lumber camp's no job for any woman. It's too hard. But it'll only be till Friday."

That's what he thought. Oh, Bill came In Friday, all right, but he was a sick man and by the time he'd recovered enough to take an interest in practical matters, the habit of Frances' authority had been established. It was to her that the cook came when he needed another crate of eggs, although she was as apt as not to say, "All right. But you're using too many eggs. I want you to cut down. There's no need of twenty-egg cake every day. Ten-egg cake is good enough." A ten-egg cake, in a lumber camp where food is prepared in pro-digious quantities and a bushel-batch is a standard frying of doughnuts, is about the equivalent of a normal two-egg cake. Frances ran the cookhouse as most housewives run their own kitchens, watching the butter and the eggs and the left-overs like a hawk, trying to establish a truce between economy and ample, appetizing meals. This sounds like the Bride's First Lesson, but it was against all woods tradition, where the food is always good and plentiful, but the waste is often terrific. Most woods cooks don't bother too much about costs. They operate on the theory that the boss is rich, and probably too busy to notice a spoiled side of mutton here or fifty pounds of lard more or less there. Frances wouldn't tolerate needless waste, and her cook knew it, but still he kept on bringing his problems to her rather than to Bill. He ended by boasting of the low-cost kitchen he ran. "Twenty-seven cents a head a day," he'd say. "And meat every meal. Can't many do better'n that." Since lumberjacks have enormous appetites, he was without doubt right.

But it wasn't only in domestic matters, which might very well come under Frances' management, that her word prevailed. Bill was still nominally the boss, but he was often away, and when a man wanted a job, it was to Frances that he applied as often as not. There is a tale about her method of hiring a man. The story is that she'd hand him her own ax, which always had an edge like a razor, and a piece of hardwood and tell him to split it fine.

"There's the chopping block," she'd say, indicating a flat block of granite near the office door. Unless he could split the wood without putting a nick in the blade, he couldn't handle an ax well enough to work for her.

"But she's fair," the woodsman who told me this tale admitted. "A joker come in the other day and wanted to be hired on. She give him the ax and the junk of firewood, like always, and he flew at it. Split it up fine as matchwood without turnin' the edge a hair, so she told him he was hired. Then he hauled off and braced his feet and brung that there ax down on the stone with all his might. It'll be a long day before that ax cuts any more wood. She was a mite put out, because naturally nobody wants their good ax ruined, so she asked him what the cryin' hell he meant by that foolishness. 'I'll tell you, ma'am,' he says, cool as you please. 'When I get through with an ax, I always leave it in the choppin' block,' and he picked up his frock and started walkin' away, because he figured he was fired before he was rightly hired. She kept him on, though. Said 'twas her own fault, that she'd asked for it."

My informant offered to show me the block of granite used as a testing ground as proof of his story, but I told him that wouldn't be necessary. I'd made up my mind at about the third sentence that it was apocryphal. But like most apocryphal tales, it had its basis in truth. Frances was a hard woman to please, and an eminently just woman in her dealings.

Whenever a new man came into camp, she herself took him up on the mountain and showed him where he was to cut. On an operation, you don't just go out and cut where you want to. You cut where the boss tells you to. The entire area has already been divided into workable units before the job starts, by the boss, who sometimes spots lines to show the divisions and sometimes carries them in his head. During the time when Bill was going to come In Friday, Frances had laid out all the cuts, so I suppose she was the logical one to take charge of that department. It does make a difference to a man where he cuts. In some places the goin' is good, as the lumberjacks say. They mean that the trees are large and bunched, so they can make a good wage at piece rates. Sometimes the goin' is lousy. The blackgrowth is scattered and interspersed with hardwood. A man can work all day hard, and never put up a full cord. In that case he may prefer to work on day, rather than piece, rates. It's not permissible to skip the poor spots and cut only where the goin' is good. When a jobber undertakes to log an area, he must cut it clean. The good jobber tries to divide his territory so that everyone has about the same chance —some good and some poor cutting. This keeps the men satisfied and reduces labor turnover, which is costly in any industry. Frances' turnover was low, so I guess she did a good job in laying out the cuts.

The telephone line which connects Middle Dam with the Outside crosses the Arm below the Greenwood camp and runs along the foot of the mountain on the west shore. One day I wanted to call up someone on the Outside, so I went up to Middle to use the Parsonses' second phone. Mine is just a woods phone, on a private wire that runs about fifteen miles from Middle Dam to the Brown Farm, and I can't talk to the Outside over it. The Parsonses have two phones, one like mine and another, beside it on the wall, that connects with Andover. It's a fascinating arrangement, especially when they both ring at the same time and you have to conduct two conversations at once, like a city editor or a movie mogul. This day I asked Al if I might use her Outside phone, and she said I could try, but it probably wouldn't do any good, as the line seemed to be out of order and was deader than a haddock.

"This is the third time this week that something's been wrong with it. Larry's gone down along the line to see if he can find the trouble. Stick around a while. He ought to be back pretty soon, and maybe he'll have fixed it."

So I stuck around, eating hot cookies and gossiping, and by and by Larry came in and threw his pliers, come-along, and other line-repairing tools on the wood-box. He was in a fine frame of mind, laughing to himself like a loony. "The line's fixed," he said. "I guess it'll stay that way now, barring Acts of God."

"What was the matter with it, and what are you giggling about?" Al wanted to know.

"Nothing special. Frances Greenwood tickles me, that's all." He picked up a handful of cookies and started eating them. "I found out what the trouble was as soon as I got down to Bill's works. The wire's strung low all the way along there, not more'n four feet off the ground, which is all right, because it's easy-reached and usually not in anybody's way. But it's too low to drive a horse under, so instead of propping it up with a pole as they ought to—there's plenty of slack; they could do it easy enough—those lazy jokers just cut it."

"Well, that's a hell of a thing to do," I commented elegantly.

"Yeah, that's what Frances thought. I was giving them my opinions on the subject when she came along. She keeps a pretty snug watch on what's going on. She's in the woods most of the time. Nobody loafs much on that job. The old she-coon's right on their tails all the time."

"The old she-coon" is not a term of disrespect in this country; or at least, I hope it's not. My children and employees often call me that when I go on the warpath. I hope it means what I think it does; the woman in charge.

"What's Bill doing all day long?" Al wanted to know, her tone bristling with sex solidarity. "Sitting home with his feet in the oven?"

"Bill's a sick man," he said. "I don't know what ails him. Maybe he's got ulcers, or diabetes, or high blood-pressure. I don't know. He looks like the Wrath-to-Come, whatever it is. Anyhow," he continued, reaching for another cookie, "along comes Frances and wants to know what the trouble is, so I told her. Did she blow her top! Climbed up one side of them and down the other. Crimus, she sure knows all the words and how to use them!" His tone was awed and respectful. "I wouldn't have dared to say the things she said to them. They'd have beat the tar out of me."

"How did they take it from her?" Al wanted to know.

"Oh, they said yes'm and no'm. Maybe it's partly because most of them wouldn't take a poke at a woman anyhow; but it's more than that, too. They're afraid of her. I don't blame them. I'm damn sure I wouldn't want to tangle with her, when she gets red-headed. She's a rugged hunk of woman, and she isn't afraid of the devil himself. That's the best-run camp I ever saw. There's less trouble there, and more work done, than in any other camp in the district. And I'll pretty near guarantee there won't be any more telephone lines cut."

And there weren't.

I stopped in there one day near the end of February. I'd been Out to see the kids, and Larry had to put in at the camp to leave the mail and some supplies. I was just as well pleased, since I was half-frozen from sitting on an open sled behind the slow-pacing horses in the sub-zero wind. Larry went into the office to deliver the mail, and I ran across the icy yard to knock on the door of the one-room shack that was Bill's and Frances' own. A voice called to me to come in, so I tore open the door, whirled inside, and slammed it behind me against the cold.

You hear a lot about Woman's Touch, and the softening influence it exercises on the most uncompromising surroundings. If this were fiction, I'd be telling you about frilled curtains at the windows of that bare little room, about geraniums blooming on window sills, and bright covers on the bunks. There'd probably be a sweet-grass sewing-basket overflowing with filmy this-and-thats somewhere around, and in all likelihood a transfigured Frances would be swishing gracefully about in a flame-colored velvet hostess gown. I'm sorry, but this is Life. The room was as bare as a barracks, and as neat. The plain gray blankets on the bunks were pulled tight and unwrinkled, the uncurtained windows shone, and you could have eaten off the floor. A few clothes hung on pegs along the wall, and in the corner by the door stood an ax, a crosscut saw, and a pair of snowshoes. There were some magazines and an ash-tray arranged neatly on a plank table, foot-lockers shoved under the bunks, and some homemade straight chairs and three-legged stools against the walls. The only wall decoration was a large poster explaining in French, English, and Russian the first principles of First Aid, and the dainty scrap of needlework in this case was a wooden cheese firkin full of rough gray socks to be mended. A large kerosene lamp with a reflector hung from the ceiling, and a little pot-bellied stove glowed cherry-red in the middle of the floor. They were the quarters of a person too busy to fuss with nonessentials, and probably too tired, at the end of the day, to do more than fall into bed.

Frances, clad in her usual costume of wool pants and a buffalo-checked shirt, was seated on a stool under the lamp, her head bent over the hand of a woodsman who was sitting on another. "This clumsy one," she said to me. "This know-nothing. First he cuts his hand and then he neglects it. No thanks to him it doesn't have to be taken off. And how would you like that, eh?" Her fingers moved gently and surely about the wound, bathing it, probing, applying salve.

The woodsman looked at me sheepishly, grimacing a little as the ointment bit. "It was an accident," he said. "Could have happened to anyone, and not worth fussin' about anyhow. Don't mind what she says. She's got an awful bark, but her bite—"

"What do you know about my bite? Have I bitten you yet? When I do, you'll know it." She started winding bandage expertly. "There, now get out of here. Vamoos. Next time you do a thing like that, you'll get your walking papers."

The woodsman picked up his hat from the floor. "She means it, too," he told me. "She don't fool around." He moved to the door. "But one thing I'll say for the old she-coon, if you're sick or hurt, she sure can be awful good to you."

"Thanks for nothing," Frances said. "What good would a camp full of cripples be to me?" But she smiled a little as the door closed behind the man. "It's good to see you, Mrs. Rich. How did you find the children?"

I said they were wonderful, and inquired for her health and Bill's. I'd seem him at the Arm when I went Out, and he didn't look at all well to me.

"Oh, me, I'm always well, like a horse. But my poor man! He can't get rid of that cough and he's miserable all over." Her eyes clouded. "The doctors don't help him. When it comes spring, I'll fix him up. I'll find the things to mend him, when the snow goes. I'll brew him up a tea that'll put hair on his chest, like my grandmother taught me." She brooded a moment and then said briskly, "Supper'll be soon. You'll stay and eat, you and Mr. Parsons?"

I said that I was sorry, but I didn't think that we could. It was already getting dark, and I'd still have two miles to snow-shoe after I got to Middle Dam, and my fire would probably be out and my house cold.

"Another time, then," she said, and I suddenly liked her a lot. She didn't try to talk me out of doing what I said I had to do, and she didn't go into a routine about "But you aren't going to walk all that way through the woods in the dark *alone!*" It was nice for once to find someone who took it for granted that I knew what I was about. I wasn't half the woman Frances Greenwood was, and I never would be; but it was heartening to have her treat me as an equal.

"She's an awfully nice woman," I said to Larry when we were out on the lake again.

"Yup, she is that. Plays a good hand of poker, too. I've been down a couple of nights to sit in on their games. She's taken two-three dollars off me. I don't like female poker players as a rule. They always want to play deuces and one-eyed Jacks wild, and that's no kind of a game. Not Frances, though. She comes across when she loses, too. Most women expect you to pay when you lose, and forget it when they do." He looked at me sideways, but I didn't rise. He could have been right. Card games bore me so that I never play them, so I wouldn't know.

Instead I said, "But how does she maintain discipline if she fraternizes with the men? If that's the heading playing poker with them comes under."

He laughed. "Don't worry about her discipline. Nobody steps over the line. Couple of weeks ago I stopped in with the mail, and I was getting my feet warm in the cookhouse when hell broke loose in the bar-room." (In the woods, that simply means the bunkhouse. For some reason the term "bunkhouse" is considered as sissified as "venison" for deer-meat and "blaze" for spot a trail.) "The cook and I went running out, but Frances was ahead of us. She busted into the bar-room with an ax-handle swinging, laying it on right and left, not bothering to ask any questions and not pulling any punches, either. When she cracked a head, she cracked a head, what I mean. She sure broke up that fight in no-time flat. I never saw a meeker bunch than that gang of hellions was when she got through with them, in about thirty seconds. She didn't waste any breath bawling them out when it was over, either. Just stood there, swinging that ax-handle in her hand and looking at them. Finally she asked, 'Anybody got anything he wants to say?' They just looked at the floor and shuffled their feet. After a minute she said, 'All right, then,' and went out and shut the door. By the time she got over to where the cook and I were standing with our mouths open, she was laughing her head off. She's a great Frances."

She certainly was. During that year and the next, three other jobbers in this vicinity went broke, but Bill Greenwood stayed in the black, and nobody had any doubts as to whom the credit belonged.

The last time I ever saw Frances Greenwood was on a March day down at South Arm. I was going to ride Out with Larry and Al to spend Easter with the children, and we'd walked the four miles down from Middle Dam on the ice, enjoying the scenery and the thin brightness of the spring sun. The thermometer stood a little above zero, but there was no wind and we were dressed in the winter uniform of the country, ski pants and sheepskins, so we were very comfortable—comfortable enough, in fact, so that we didn't stop in at Greenwoods' to get warm, as we usually did. We saw sled tracks leading across the snow from the camp to the Arm, so we concluded that some of the crew must be going Out, too; and when we were about half a mile from Larry's landing, we saw a cluster of black specks that were people milling around the garages. As we drew nearer, Al snatched off her sunglasses, which we all wear as protection against the terrible glare from the snow.

"Hey, Louise," she said. "Am I going woods queer at last, or do you see what I see?"

I looked, and took off my glasses and looked again. "Who in the world—? Al, if anyone's crazy, it isn't us. Where did she come from? She'd better go back there, wherever it is, before she dies of exposure." Because we were looking at a very smartly dressed woman, a sight to see indeed on the shore of the Arm in the winter. She had on a sheered beaver jacket, a dark wool dress, and a silly and enchanting little hat all covered with flowers.

"Hello," she said, and then we saw that it was Frances Greenwood. She'd let her hair grow, and now it wasn't crowwing black any more, but streaked with gray. She looked very distinguished indeed, as though she were Somebody—as in fact she was, if anybody ever was.

"We didn't know you in your Outside clothes," I said. "You look lovely!"

"Thank you." She smoothed her white suede gloves. "I feel foolish. It's been so long since I've worn regular clothes, but we're going down to spend Easter with our son, and I don't want him to be ashamed before his wife's folks." She laughed and looked down at her sheer silk stockings. "I feel as if I was naked, after wearing breeches all winter."

"Aren't you cold?" I asked, but she said she wasn't. She'd come down on the sled, wrapped in blankets.

"The camp's about closed," she said. "The clerk can finish up. We won't be In again."

"But we'll see you next year!" Al exclaimed.

"No, we won't be back at all. We've decided to get out of the logging business. We've done pretty well, and we've saved some money. We're buying a boarding house down-country, and we're going to run that for a change. It'll be a lot easier."

Al and I said that that was fine; that the life she had been leading was much too hard for any woman.

Just then Bill joined us to say that he had the car shoveled out of the garage and ready to go. I'd never happened to have seen him and Frances together before, and I was surprised at the way Frances looked up at him with eyes as soft and liquid as a doe's, and a little wild-rose flush on her high cheek-bones.

"That's what the Boss says," she told us. "I wanted to go on for at least another winter. I don't mind life in a camp. But the Boss says, 'Let the company finish the cut.' He says it's time I had it easier, and what the Boss says, goes." And Bill's chest expansion increased by inches as he took her arm to help her over the roughness of the road; to help Frances Green-wood, the old she-coon, who could cross the worst ridge in the country faster than any man alive, over a few measly little ruts and humps of snow!

"We'll miss you!" Al and I called after her truthfully, and then we looked at each other and back to where she was cling-ing to his arm, picking her way and exclaiming fearfully and smiling up into his face. We didn't have to say what was in both our minds. There was no doubt about it at all. Frances Greenwood was a smart woman.

10

A Policeman's Lot

IN THIS COUNTRY, we are probably the least policed group of people in the world, with the possible exception of the native tribes back in the hills of places like New Guinea. Our conduct—like theirs, I presume—is governed by expediency and our own good sense, rather than by the outside pressure of the law. It isn't very sensible or expedient to subject your neighbor to murder, theft, or arson, just because he can't yell for the cop on the corner. He could turn right around and do even worse to you, and obviously a state of anarchy would soon ensue, in which nobody would be either safe or happy. We practice the doctrine of do unto others, not because of religious conviction, but because we have found it to be the only rule under which a reasonably good life is possible. We don't necessarily have to love our neighbors, but we do have to treat them decently; and it is an interesting fact that usually the people whom you start out by being decent to on principle, you end by liking in practice. I don't know whether this system would work on a universal scale or not, and since there is very little likelihood of the experiment's being tried, I'm not bothering my head about it. It's enough for me that it works here.

Of course, we are technically subject to the general law of the State of Maine, so once in a while we have to evoke the legal forces. In the case of a violent or sudden death, for example, we have to call the sheriff and the coroner. This sounds a little terrifying, but since the sheriff is Bob Milton, whom we've all known for years, and the coroner is nice old Dr. Greene, who has seen the children through infected blisters and tonsilitis, you can dismiss whatever pictures of police grillings have been forming in your mind. With perfect courtesy and great consideration, they ask whatever questions are pertinent, formulate their opinion, and go back to where they came from. The only other officers of the law we ever see are the game and fire wardens, and in winter, when the woods are so deep under snow that you couldn't start a forest fire if you tried, we don't even have a fire warden.

For a while I was in the bad graces of our game warden, Leon Wilson, because I once stated in the public prints that he was handsome and romantic-looking. I don't think he believed that I was buttering him up so that he would take a broad-minded view of any infractions of the law I might be contemplating. And I wasn't either. In the first place, I knew better. Any time he thought I needed it, he'd just as soon arrest me as look at me; me, or the President of the United States. In the second place, among the few laws of the land that I wouldn't break if I felt like it and thought I could get away with it are the game laws. I believe in them. No, the reason he objected to my remarks was purely professional. He felt that I had undermined his authority. He didn't like having incipient poachers addressing him as Glamour-puss or Gorgeous. I'd feel a lot worse about the whole thing if I thought I had really done him an injury. As it happens, I am perfectly confident that he can handle with neatness and dispatch any situation which might arise from my remarks. All I was trying to do at the time of writing was a piece of accurate reporting.

That's what I'm still trying to do, so I guess I'll have to jeopardize our re-established amicable relations by saying again that I think Leon is handsome. He is tall and lean and dark, with a tough, competent, hard-bitten way about him, and he wears his uniform with a swashbuckling air. He looks like a modern pirate, but actually he is the father of four, including a pair of twins, and a conscientious, capable, indefatigable officer of the law. His official duties, as far as the Parsonses and I are concerned, aren't too wearing. The first time after New Year's that he sees us, he writes down the numbers of our new guides' licenses, which carry with them hunting and fishing privileges, in his little black note-book. This is so that we won't have to carry them with us for the rest of the year, as the law insists. It's an obvious legal provision, but in our cases not a very practical one. Most of us are continually falling into the river by mistake or wading into the lake on purpose to help launch a boat, and any documents in our hip pockets would shortly disintegrate under that treatment. As Leon once pointed out to me, it is not his business to make people's lives miserable over the picayune letter of the law, but to see that the spirit is observed. This was on an occasion when I had hooked and landed a short salmon, and he happened to be present.

Usually a fish is hooked through the membrane surrounding its mouth, a thin, tough, parchment-like tissue without any blood veins in it, and can be taken off the hook with no damage done to it. Occasionally, as in this case, the hook penetrates the flesh and it's impossible to remove it without causing bleeding. I said to Leon, "I suppose I've got to throw this fish back, since it's under legal size; but I might as well tell you right now that if you weren't here, I'd keep it. It's bleeding, and it's going to die anyhow." Even if a fish is bleeding only a little, it does die very soon after you return it to the water, and floats belly-up and malodorous in some back eddy until it rots away.

He inspected the fish. "I guess it is," he said. "That being the case, you might as well kill it and get· some good out of it, instead of having it go to waste." So I tapped it smartly at the base of the skull with a sheath-knife handle, and cooked and ate it for lunch. That's what I call being a sensible cop.

Once he has taken our license numbers, Leon can wipe off his official expression, sit down with a cup of coffee, relax and tell us the news. He covers a large territory and has sources of information denied us, isolated as we are. He knows who isn't speaking to whom in Upton and why, and where those people who used to live on the Byron Road moved to. We consider him a friend who happens to wear a uniform, rather than a policeman; and in my case, the fact that I once bought a secondhand kerosene refrigerator from his mother-in-law, through his kind offices, forms a sort of third-cousinly family tie. He annually inquires, for the former owner, as to the health of the refrigerator; and since I can always report happily that it never causes me a moment's worry and is the best buy I ever made, as I honestly don't know how I'd get along without it, an aura of general good feeling is generated. Then I start picking his brains, because in my business gold is where you find it, and he knows and has done a lot of things that I can use. He's aware of my intentions, but he doesn't seem to mind. I once wrote a book for teen-age boys, based partly on stories that Leon had told me. It was kindly received by reviewers and actually won a literary prize, which I found extremely gratifying. My real triumph came, however, when Leon read it and informed me that he hadn't found one technical or factual error in it. I was *really* set up about that.

When Leon was young and didn't know any better, so he says, he was one of the worst poachers in the State of Maine. At that time he lived up near Fort Kent, along the Canadian border, and if anyone thinks it's uncivilized where we live, he ought to go up there. That's really wild country, so wild that even the wardens pay no attention to the Sunday hunting law. Most of the time they don't even know it's Sunday; and if they did, it wouldn't make any difference. The Sunday law isn't necessary up there. It's not a blue law, contrary to common belief, but simply a precautionary measure against race suicide. Sunday is the only day that lots of people are free to hunt—people who work in mills and offices—and but for the Sunday law, the woods would be full of trigger-happy individuals, popping away at anything that stirred without stopping to determine whether it was four-legged, two-legged, or merely a breeze in a bush. This law is a little hard on the regularly employed lovers of the chase, but not as hard as a bullet through the head would be. The woods along the border, though, are too remote to be accessible to Sunday-only hunters, so the law has been allowed to fall more or less into abeyance.

But the classes with more leisure at their disposal can and do take time off to go on a week's hunting trip that far from the beaten track. Sometimes they are not too successful in bagging any quarry, so on the day before they must start for home, they'll go looking for an amenable native who will sell them a deer. This is strictly against the law, and all parties involved are liable to severe punishment if caught. However, since the price of a deer is ten dollars and up, and since ten dollars is a lot of money back here in the sticks, a lively traffic in dead deer does exist, and Leon used to be an especially successful operator. He told me once that it is one of the seven wonders of the modern world that he was never caught. He used to have as many as six or eight deer strung up on a cross-pole just a little way back in the forest from where he lived, and if anyone came asking to buy one, he'd take them out there and let them have their pick. He didn't bother much about their credentials, but simply trusted to instinct to warn him which strangers were all right and which were either disguised officers or stool pigeons. He was just lucky that his instinct was so good.

Finally, in desperation possibly, the V.I.P.'s decided to put him on the other side of the fence by making him a warden. Probably they figured, so Leon says, that there's nothing like setting a thief to catch a thief, so to speak, and this time they were absolutely right. His really extraordinary talents, diverted into the channels of the right, and the instinct that used to inform him when the law was near now just as unerringly communicates the presence of lawlessness to him. Of people who look and act like perfectly upright citizens to me, he will say, "I don't know what they're up to *yet*, but there's something off-color there." Sooner or later he catches them with the evidence upon them. Then some thuggish-looking character whom I wouldn't trust around the first bend in the river comes along, and Leon says, "Him? He's okay." And it turns out that he is. I don't know how

Leon does it, but I suspect that he smells poachers, just as a dog can tell by the sense of smell who is afraid of him.

But all this was a long time ago and is probably just as well forgotten, except that it illustrates the point that once a renegade doesn't necessarily mean always a renegade. Leon continued as a good and able warden up along the Allegash and St. John rivers until the day came, as it must to all of us backwoods parents, when his children reached school age. We are then, all of us, faced with a choice of parting with our offspring for ten months of the year—if we can find a suitable place for them to live, with wise and responsible people, which is not as easy as it may sound—or of moving with them to civilization. The Wilsons chose to move, so Leon asked for a transfer, and now they live over in Newry. I think he still feels a little homesick for the border, judging by the way he talks about life up there. He sounds exactly the way I feel when I'm away from here and get to thinking that the river is still curling over the ledges, and the big mossy rock by my door still acts as pivot for its arcing shadow as the sun goes over from east to west, and the pines across the rapids still toss their cone-heavy heads against the windy sky, and I'm not there to see. It's a desolate feeling, and he has my sympathy. What he misses most, I guess, is his dogs. Up in that country the warden uses a dog team to get around in winter, but of course in this time and place that isn't necessary; and I don't care what anyone says, you simply cannot become as attached to a jeep as you can to a bunch of big, vicious-looking, loving-hearted huskies. I know, because I used to have a dog team myself, and I adored every one of the brutes.

The game warden's duties consist primarily of seeing that the game laws are observed, and I would say, off-hand, that

that is a full-time job for any man. Maine is a comparatively poor state and can't afford battalions of wardens, so each man's territory is pretty large and, up here where there are no roads, difficult to cover. He has to depend on canoes to a large extent, and on his feet even more. To complicate matters, it is extremely desirable that he remain as nearly invisible as is possible for the corporeal; so he wastes a great deal of time hiding in thickets or lying flat in swamps, so that the news of his presence in the neighborhood won't be broadcast. By certain elements he is considered Public Enemy Number One, and if he is sighted, the grapevine gets to work.

I was down at the Foot-of-the-Falls one morning, hauling out a canoe that I'd left there, when I saw written in letters three feet tall on a sand bar, for anyone who might be interested to read, "WARDEN UP THE RIVER." It was impossible for anyone landing a boat at the head of the slack water or walking along the bank to miss it. I went home, and late that afternoon Leon came knocking at the kitchen door to see if he could have supper with us.

"Oh, hello," I said. "I've been expecting you."

"And why would you be expecting me? I'm supposed to be over at Sturtevant Pond. At least, I've tried hard to give that impression."

I told him, and the air was pretty blue for a few minutes. Finally he simmered down enough to make sense. "God damn it," he said, "I'd like to know who saw me. I've been after a certain party all summer, and when I found out that they were planning to fish the Rapid River to-day, I thought for sure my time had come. I spent half the night walking through the woods from over in New Hampshire and the rest of it Indian-paddling in the pitch dark across Umbagog. Then I've been lying in the bushes and rocks all day long without a thing to eat, getting cricks in my back and being chewed up by black flies, all for nothing. The party I'm after acted like a bunch of preachers, bending over backward to stay inside the law, when ordinarily they're the damnedest poachers unhung. I knew it wasn't natural, but I couldn't figure out how they could have been tipped off. When I find out who wrote that, I'll—" His discourse reverted to the unprintable, and I learned about several forms of torture that had never come to my attention before.

On the other hand, one October day I was up at Middle Dam visiting with Al Parsons when Leon blew in. "Well, for the love of peace," I said. "The Law, by gum. Hel-*lo*! I haven't laid eyes on a warden since August. I thought you were dead."

"The warden's laid eyes on you, though," he told me in a rather sinister manner. "Several times."

I passed my activities since August in quick mental review and decided that I dared to ask, "What was I doing?"

"Never mind what you were doing," he said darkly. "You weren't breaking the law, anyhow, or you'd have soon found out I was around." That's all he'd tell me, and I don't know yet, and never will know, what I was doing under his surveillance. A good warden keeps his affairs to himself.

The work is hard enough during the fishing season, but it gets harder after the hunting season opens. Then the warden has to work at night as well as during the daytime. An easy, but illegal, way to shoot a deer is to sneak into an old orchard or field after dark with a jack-light, lie in hiding until the deer come down to feed, then turn on the light—

usually a seven-cell flashlight with a reflector—and shoot the deer as he stands bewitched and bedazzled in the glare. This is completely unsporting, of course, besides being unlawful, and arouses the warden's humane, as well as his professional, instincts. So all through the long fall he spends his nights lying out on the frosty ground, courting pneumonia and rheumatism. He also catches quite a grist of malefactors, which is what makes the game worth the candle.

We had an inveterate and highly talented poacher in our midst a few years ago, whom I will call Morgan Twitchell. Leon knew what he was up to, all right, but he was never able to catch him red-handed, a fact which drove him mad with outraged pride. He spent a great deal of time on Morgan, laying traps for him, following him around, and using all his skill to bring him to book. Finally, acting on information and a sixth sense of his own, he had a warrant sworn out and searched the Twitchell home, finding there enough evidence in the form of untagged deer to put Morgan in jail for the rest of the season. Morgan wasn't at home at the time, and he was as well endowed with sixth senses as Leon. Sniffing danger—that's the only way I can account for it—he circled around his house and vanished into the blue. He could have been a wonderful warden, himself; but he was truly incorrigible. He preferred to break the law, to satisfy some craving for adventure, I suppose, and would rather poach a half-starved rabbit than kill legally the fattest buck that ever ran the woods.

A great hue and cry was raised, and everyone for miles around speculated for days as to the whereabouts of Morgan Twitchell, including Catherine, who was working for me, and me. I was spending the weekend out at Rumford Point, where we had rented a house so that the children could attend school, and we were whiling away a Sunday afternoon sitting in the living-room, talking. I said, "I'd just like to know where Morgan is right now." I knew him and I rather liked him. He was a personable and obliging and merry young man, aside from his lawless proclivities.

"Well," Catherine said thoughtfully, staring out the window, "if you *really* want to know, he's just driving into our driveway."

"You're not even a clever liar," I told her, because it didn't seem to me to be very smart to tell a lie that could be quickly exposed by my simply turning my head and looking out the window myself. So I did look out, and there was Morgan crossing the lawn unhurriedly with his wife and son. They knocked at the door and came in, laughing at our exclamations.

"First," said Morgan, "where's the back door, in case I have to leave in a hurry? And second, may we use your telephone? We've been over calling on some relatives in Milton Plantation, and my wife left her glasses there. We want to ask them if they'll mail them to-morrow." The second part of his speech was so at odds with the first, and with my ideas of what a fugitive from justice should have on his mind, that I burst into helpless laughter. When that was over and the phone call had been completed, we sat down to visit over cups of coffee.

"But where have you been?" I asked. "Every warden in three counties has been looking for you for days."

"Sure, I know it. I've seen them. I'll tell you how to keep from being arrested, if you want. Who knows? It might come in handy for you to know sometime. You just find out where the cops are and start following *them* around. They never think to look behind them. I've been on their tails ever since Friday night."

"That's all very well," I said, unimpressed. "But it can't go on forever. Sooner or later, probably sooner, they're going to catch you, so I can't see what you're gaining by playing games with them."

"Oh, sure they'll catch me. I know that. But what I'm gaining is time. I don't want to be pinched until Tuesday," Morgan explained with sweet reasonableness. I've known about some strange compromises with the law since I came to Maine to live, including the case of a çasual acquaintance of mine from the next county, whom the sheriff wouldn't arrest for murder until after the sheriff's daughter's marriage, because the suspect was going to be best man, and his arrest would upset the wedding plans and give the mother of the bride one of her famous sick headaches. But I didn't see at first glance why it should make any difference to Morgan whether he were arrested right that minute or two days later, and I said so.

"Well, you see, I haven't tagged my deer yet." We tacitly omitted any reference to the untagged deer found in his house. They'd been confiscated, anyhow. "As soon as they get me, they'll suspend my license until my case comes up in court. If I'm found guilty, they'll take it away altogether, and I can't hunt any more this year. I want a deer to see us through the winter. I can't hunt to-day, with them so hot on my trail, but if I can have to-morrow to hunt legally, I'll guarantee to get my deer. Then I don't care what they do to me."

Morgan overestimated his skill or luck. He didn't get his

deer Monday, and Tuesday they arrested him anyhow. However, his case was dismissed on a legal technicality—poachers usually know more about the law and its loopholes than lawyers do—and he was set free, presumably to continue his evil practices. A week later I saw Leon, who didn't seem to be as full of wrath and frustration as I had anticipated. I'd expected him to be frothing at the mouth at the latest proof of Morgan's wiliness.

"He's not going to be bothering me any more this season," Leon explained. "Didn't you hear? He broke his leg in two places day before yesterday, down at the birch mill. That'll keep him quiet for a while. You know, Louise, sometimes I think there is a certain amount of justice in life, after all."

He crowed too soon. Two weeks later Morgan was riding along in his car with his rifle beside him, not because he hoped to use it but because he felt undressed without it, when a big bear ambled out into the road. Morgan pulled on the hand brake, reached for his crutches, maneuvered himself into the road, loaded his gun, and put a bullet between the animal's eyes. It was a perfectly legal proceeding; but what made Leon speechless with rage was that Morgan collected the usual twenty-five dollar bounty on bear. This Leon thought was adding insult to injury, and I can see how he felt.

The wardens' duties don't end with enforcing the game laws. Among other things they have to check periodically on empty camps to see that they haven't been broken into, recover stolen property like guns and boats, assist the fire wardens and immigration authorities when necessary, and search for lost persons. It keeps them pretty busy, and I am inclined to agree that the policeman's lot, at times, is indeed not a happy one, even if it is occasionally colorful and exciting. One case Leon had a few years ago especially fired my imagination, and I haven't got over it yet.

At that time Bill and Frances Greenwood were running their logging operation down in South Arm, and late one stormy night the clerk came in with thirteen woodsmen that he'd gone Outside to hire. In accordance with custom, he'd found them by making a survey of the bar-rooms and beer joints of the nearest large town, and of course they were all roaring drunk. It was not only dark, but bitterly cold, with a terrible wind driving the snow straight down the lake. The clerk, who was sober, knew that he would never be able to walk his charges the mile across the ice to camp that night, so he herded them into a cabin on the east shore, built them up a good fire, put the least intoxicated man in charge, and went over to get a good night's sleep in his own bed at camp. He needed it after the day he'd put in with his drunks, and he felt sure they'd be all right until someone came over to get them with a sled in the morning.

In the morning there were only twelve men there. The clerk had not made a mistake in counting. He was cold sober, and he wasn't the kind of man who makes mistakes like that. Nobody could have walked back to civilization on a night like that, even if he'd been sober and fresh; and anyhow the missing man never showed up in Andover, the first village. He couldn't have fallen into the lake, because the ice was thirty inches thick, with no holes in it. The only conclusion possible was that he'd gone outside the cabin, become confused, and just wandered around until he was overcome with cold and exhaustion. So Bill Greenwood started yelling for the warden.

The man was never found. Every drift on the lake was

investigated, in spite of the crotch-deep snow; the woods were scoured for two miles around the cabin, and the high banks of snow on both sides of the road were levelled all the way to Cedar Hill. No trace of him was uncovered. It then became the warden's business to send out word asking any-one who knew of the man's whereabouts—or the man himself, in case by some miracle he had survived to gain the Outside—to communicate with the authorities; and here he arrived at another impasse. No one knew who the man was. Usually the woodsmen all know each other. They run into each other continually on various operations or in the bars and dives of the towns where they spend the off-season. But no one had ever seen this man before. Sure, they remembered his being with them in the truck on the way to the lake; and they gave more or less consistent descriptions of him. But no one could remember just when or where he had joined the party, no one had any idea what his name was or where he came from, and everyone insisted that he couldn't have left the cabin at all, because they had a chair wedged under the door latch to keep the wind from blowing it open.

That's all there is to that story. Of course, the woodsmen believe that he wasn't a mortal man at all, and there are times when I'm not sure that I believe he was, either. This is such a strange, wild country, and sometimes when the wind is moaning up the river and the ghostly fingers of the sleet are tapping on the windows— But that's the purest nonsense, of course, considered in the sane light of day! The facts are queer enough without embroidery. *Who* was he, this thir-teenth man whose orbit touched ours so briefly; what manner of man? What did he think about, and what was important to him? Where did he go? The problem seduces my mind into endless speculation.

When I first knew Leon, I used to be shy of him. He was so tough and hard-boiled and business-like. He'd come to the door with a look on his face that immediately convinced me that I was guilty. I certainly felt ill-at-ease and constrained enough. After about two years of telling myself not to be silly, that my strength ought to be as the strength of ten because my heart was pure, I got over blushing and stammering whenever I saw him; but I still couldn't feel exactly matey toward him. He seemed so cold-blooded and ruthless and inhuman. And then the Squareheads moved into the Notch.

Grafton Notch is a forbidding place that greatly intrigues me, although I'm happy to say that my experience with it is limited. It's a high pass in the mountains that you have to go over in order to get from the valley of the Androscoggin to the basin of Umbagog. A brook threads through it, and there are starved fields and abandoned orchards and deserted farms squeezed against the road by the towering cliffs on either side. Once it was inhabited, but the early settlers were driven out by the impossibility of making a living there, which has always seemed sad to me. They worked so hard, clearing the land and building their stone walls and low farmhouses; and then even the seasons betrayed them. They discovered that because of the altitude and the walls of the mountains cutting off the sun for all except a few hours in the middle of the day, not a month of the year goes by without bringing a black, killing frost to the Notch. So they had to move away, leaving their homes and their hopes behind them. Most of the buildings have long since fallen down, but one or two of the more sturdily built still stand, their cedar shingles black and curling, their broken windows gaping idiotically. It was into one of these that the Squareheads moved.

What their name really was I never knew, nor what their nationality. In this country, everyone who isn't a Yankee or a French-Canadian is a Squarehead. The family consisted of a mother and father and a large brood of children ranging from almost man-grown down to a toddler of about three, who was not, so Leon reported to me, too young to cut seed potatoes and help clear the gullied and overgrown fields of the smaller stones and bushes. They had a few hens and ducks, a scrubby little cow, a team of gaunt old horses, and not much else in the line of possessions with which to bless themselves.

"They've got their courage with them, that I will say," Leon told me, "trying to make a go of farming that rock-heap. I'll give them credit, they certainly know what work means. They're at it all day long and half into the night, and considering that they've got almost nothing to do with, they're accomplishing an awful lot. But you know what the Notch is. It takes more than work to make a living there. It would take a crying miracle. I'd almost feel sorry for them, except—"

"Except what?"

"I wish I knew. There's something wrong with them. People with clear consciences don't act the way they do. I sure as hell would like to know what they've got on their minds. It must be something pretty bad, the way they act."

"How do you mean, the way they act?" I demanded, and he shrugged his shoulders.

"I can't tell you. It's nothing you can put your finger on.

It's just the way they look at me, answering my questions like butter wouldn't melt in their mouths. You know yourself that's not natural, not unless they're hiding something. Oh, well, give me time; I'll find out what it is. I haven't started giving them the real working-over yet."

The next time I saw him, a few weeks later, I asked him about the Squareheads, more to make conversation than anything else. We were sitting on the porch at Forest Lodge with our feet on the deacon seat that runs along the rail, smoking and watching the river tumble down-hill. He brought his feet down with a crash and spat over the pole railing.

"Those so-and-sos!" he said savagely. "I came damn near beating up that oldest son of theirs the other day, regulations or no regulations. Nobody can pull a knife on me and make me like it. Nothing makes me madder, except being shot at. I suppose that'll be the next thing. Maybe I ought to go back and pound the tar out of him anyhow, on general principles."

"Pulled a knife on you! Why, Leon, that's—that's—" I sputtered into shocked silence.

"I'll tell you how it was. I was following the brook up the Notch, when I stumbled onto one of the middle young-ones— twelve or so, he is—fishing one of the pools. He was fishing legal, all right; but this year that brook is closed. I latched onto him and started up to the house, holding him by the arm because he'd tried to run away. I wasn't going to do anything about it, except warn the old man. That brook's been open so long I figured maybe they didn't realize they weren't supposed to fish it this year. I've caught a lot of folks in there since spring, and the first time I always let them go with a warning, things being as they are. I aimed to be fair and give the Squareheads the same chance as I would anyone else, much as I don't like them. And besides, to be honest with you, I didn't want to mess around with a piddling little thing like a kid fishing a closed stream. I'm waiting to get them on something really serious. And I will, too."

He brooded for a minute. "Anyhow, when we got up near the barn where the old man and the biggest boy were mending harness, the kid started to scream and jabber something in that outlandish language of theirs. Did I tell you they don't speak English very well? Well, they don't, except the old man. He's not so bad. So the kid starts screaming—sounded like he was warning them about something—and I gave him a little shake to shut him up. I didn't hurt him, honest! But the big boy reaches for his knife.

"I got set for trouble, let me tell you. But the old man snapped something in his own language, and the boy sort of hesitated and then made out like he was just going to cut a piece of strap with the knife. He didn't fool me any, but there wasn't much I could do. The old man put on that smooth face of his and started apologizing for the kid before he'd even found out what he'd done. You know yourself, Louise, that isn't the way people act normally. I explained the situation, and he palavered around a while, waving his hands and almost busting into tears, till I got sick of it and left. But don't worry; I'll go back. They can't always be lucky."

But time went on, and I didn't learn about anything untowards happening to the Squareheads in the Notch, although I read the Police News in the local paper religiously every week, as I always do to see if any of my friends among the lumberjacks have fallen afoul of the law. Leon himself I didn't see for a long time, as much as six weeks or so, and by the time he drifted in one autumn day, I'd almost forgotten the whole affair. Finally, though, I did think to inquire, "How are your pals over in the Notch?"

"Oh, them." To my surprise, he started to laugh with genuine good humor. "I found out what ailed them at last, thank God. It was getting me down, not being able to pin something on anybody as guilty-acting as they were. I began to think I was slipping and ought to turn in my badge."

"For Heaven's sake, what was it?"

"It's a long story, and you're not going to believe it. I didn't myself at first. I never ran into anything quite like it, and— Well, to start with, right after I saw you last I began a sort of war of nerves, like you're always reading about in the papers nowadays. I'd show up at funny times in funny places, sometimes a couple of times a day for a spell. Then I'd leave them alone for a while, and then I'd be living in their back pockets again. I figured that if I got them edgy enough, they'd be sure to make a break. And by God, they did. I walked into their kitchen one morning at about five o'clock, while they were eating breakfast—they begin the day early—and just stood looking at them."

I could well imagine that look, and I cringed in sympathy with the Squareheads. Leon doesn't realize, I guess, how well he can impersonate righteous and terrible retribution.

"They just froze in their tracks," he went on. "One kid had a spoonful of mush halfway to her mouth, and it just stayed there with the milk dropping off into the dish, slow. The biggest boy looked right at me, and if anybody ever hated my guts— He had his hands on the table, and the fingers started to curl as if he had hold of my throat. The old man just got whiter and whiter. It sort of fascinated me, to see anybody get that white. The old lady was the one that broke down. All of a sudden she started crying and carrying on. I couldn't understand what she was saying, of course, but the old man got up and patted her on the shoulder and talked to her, and in a minute she calmed down a little. To tell the truth, I was beginning to wish I was somewhere else. I didn't actually have a thing on them, when you came right down to it, except *knowing* there was something wrong with them; and you can't take that kind of evidence into court, not if you don't want the judge splitting his sides laughing at you. Just as I was wondering what I was supposed to do next, the old boy took matters in his own hands.

"He straightened up and looked at me and started talking. It was the first time I ever saw him without that hound-dog look on his face, or heard him speak without apologizing all over the place about nothing, and it made a lot of difference. He started out on the wrong foot, though. He said he didn't know what I was after, because they didn't have any money; but if I'd just go away and leave them alone, I could have the cow and those old crow-bait horses.

"That made me mad. It always does, when someone offers me a five spot to forget about a short fish or an unstamped beaver pelt. Sweet Simon, what's the point of having wardens if you can buy them off? So I told him I didn't want his jeesley livestock or anything else that belonged to him, and what was more, I had a good mind to run him in for trying to bribe an officer. I laid it on thick, because I was pretty disgusted. I told him I didn't know how it was where he came from, but here you couldn't get away with that stuff, and the sooner he realized it the better for him. I said people who

kept their noses clean didn't go around offering bribes, because they knew there was no need of it. Then I asked him
if he had anything to say for himself.

"For once he did. It was queer. He stood there with
tears running down his face, but for once he didn't act
afraid of me. He said— Oh, I can't put it in his words, because he talks funny, sort of broken English with an accent,
but educated, like he'd learned it out of a book. But the gist
of it was that there wasn't one damn thing I could do to
them." Leon laughed. "That's the kind of talk I can understand. I get it all the time, and sometimes it's true, but oftener
it isn't. I started to blast him, like I would anybody, but he
held up his hand and I shut up." He looked a little surprised.
"I don't know why, but I did, and he went on raving. He said
they'd been chased from country to country over across, and
somewhere along the line one of his sons had been killed
and his mother and oldest girl taken away, and at last they'd
managed somehow to get to this country. He thought they'd
be all right here, and could live in peace without men in
big black boots with guns on their hips busting into their
house at all hours of the day and night—"

Leon looked at his beautifully polished boots, propped
on the fender, and at the heavy revolver in its holster as if
they didn't belong to him. He shook his head, and after a
minute went on. "He said he didn't give a damn what I did,
that nothing I could cook up would be any worse than what
they'd already had. I could torture them and kill them and
burn their buildings, but he wasn't going to run away again.
There wasn't any place left to run to, if this country was
rotten too, and he'd rather be dead anyhow than live in a
world where there was no room for innocent people who only

wanted to be left alone. I thought he was kidding—about me torturing them, I mean—but by God, he wasn't. He believed I might, and he really didn't care."

He sat looking into the open fire for a long minute. "I knew all along there was something awful wrong with that bunch; but hell, Louise, how could I guess? You read about people being persecuted, and you know it's true, but you don't really *believe* it. I've had plenty of guys afraid of me in my time, for the good reason that they damn well knew they were off-side the law; and I enjoyed making them sweat. They had it coming to them. But I never ran across anyone before who was just plain *afraid*. It sort of threw me off. It was something I couldn't understand."

I looked at him, and suddenly I liked him better than I ever had before, because he really was the sort of person who couldn't understand how such a terrible thing could be, how a clear conscience could possibly fail to drive out fear. "How are you getting along with them now?" I asked.

He laughed. "Oh, swell. I drop in there once in a while and stay for a meal. The old lady's a good cook, though she does stir up some awful funny foreign dishes. Good, though, for a change. I'm going to miss them when they're gone."

"Gone?" I said blankly. "But I thought they refused to move again."

"They're not going far. They've begun to realize what the Notch is like, so when I heard about this old farm down below Sumner, going cheap at a tax sale, I told the old man. 'Tisn't much, pretty run-down, but compared to what they've got— The way they all sail into a job of work, they'll have a nice place there in a few years. They're going to move before snowfall. They're out of my district over there, but I guess they'll be all right. The last time I saw them I had to bawl one of the kids out for tickling trout, and he answered me back sassy, just like any kid."

"What did you do then?" I asked, laughing.

"What do you think? I climbed up one side of him and down the other, and threatened to throw him in the can. I wouldn't have, of course. He wasn't doing any real harm. Anyhow, I felt too good about him talking back to me so natural to get really nasty with him." He took his feet down, rose to his considerable height, settled his holster, and tightened his belt. "Well, I've got to shove along. Guess I'll go up to Upper Dam and see what I can uncover in the line of a crime wave there."

And he went off up the Carry, striding along and looking very tough and hard-boiled and ruthless, and even a little bit cold-blooded and inhuman.

11

The Hired Help

RIGHT AT THE start let's have it clearly understood that up here in the backwoods there is no such thing as a servant, in the popular sense. Those persons employed in the households of others are the hired help, and there is a vast difference between being one of the help and being a servant, the difference implicit in the two terms. In the course of seventeen years of living in this country, I have employed probably a dozen different individuals, and in no case can a person be said to have *served* me. Rather they have *helped* me. We have worked together on an equal footing, exchanging the two equally valuable commodities of labor and money, to the end of furthering the common welfare. Somewhere Cervantes remarked, "One of the most considerable advantages the great have over their inferiors is to have servants as good as themselves." My only claim to greatness lies in the fact that the rest of the remark certainly applies to my situation. My hired help has invariably been as good as I am, from any point of view, and in some cases, I'll have to admit, a whole lot better.

That's the way it has to be in this country, because simple geography makes the spending together of most of the waking hours compulsory for people living under the same roof.

In towns and cities on the maid's night out, she can go to the movies or over to see her girl-friend. Here there simply isn't anywhere to go, no form of easy entertainment, and nobody to see. After the supper dishes are dried, there's nothing to do except go into the living room and read or sew or play cribbage or talk. Therefore a very sound principle to follow in hiring help in the backwoods is that anyone who isn't good enough to eat at the same table and sit in the same living room with you just isn't good enough to work for you in the first place. The rule has rather an arbitrary sound, but it works out very well. Of all the people I've ever hired, I've only had to fire one man.

I was sorry about that for two reasons. The first one was that the necessity for firing him showed that my judgment was not infallible, a fact that I hated to admit. The other was that we really liked him. He was good-natured and willing and truly amusing. He had a quick wit and a lively intelligence and true acting ability. We never laughed so hard as during the time Etienne worked for us and enlivened our mealtimes with his exuberant and dramatic re-enactments of various episodes in his career. But unfortunately he was not very reliable. We parted company after a few weeks, and we've never seen him since.

We remember him, though, every time something too much to be borne with equanimity happens. Then someone says viciously, "Astramonia!" hissing the *s* and bearing down, tight-lipped, on the *m*. That was an oath of Etienne's, which we all picked up. He told us that it was Polish and all right for us to use, since it didn't mean anything worse than son-of-a-bitch, which is one of the milder imprecations of this country; and it sounds better, too. I hope he was telling the truth, but I wouldn't bet money on it. Etienne had the kind of sense of humor that might easily have led him into thinking it very funny to hear Gertie Roberts, who was also working for me at the time and who is a pillar of respectability and looks it, ripping out a really nasty word, in all innocence. If that is the case, I only hope nobody who understands Polish happens along in one of our crises. Be that as it may, I am grateful to Etienne for Astramonia. When things get bad enough to call for its use, the next step is either demoralizing tears or helpless laughter, and Astramonia always tips the scales in favor of the tension-relieving laughter.

Of the others who have worked for me, one, Gerrish, of whom I have written before, I lost by death. All the rest left when the job in hand was done, or when September came and the kids had to go Out to school, and I didn't need help any more. We always parted friends, and I do truly mean friends, on a corresponding, visiting-back-and-forth, truly-interested-in-each-others'-affairs basis; that is, all except two men whose names I never did know, who once worked for me for a week in the spring. Brief as our contract was, and in spite of the fact that we never exchanged one word that was intelligible to me, at least, I'll never forget them.

This is the way it happened. It was May, and the ice had just gone out, and the log-drive had started. I'd been living alone all winter, contented as a well-fed woodchuck with the world in general. Then one day Al Parsons called me up to remind me that the Siases, dear friends of mine, were arriving in two days to stay at the hotel for the spring fishing. I went outdoors and suddenly saw the familiar yard through their eyes, or the eyes of any Outsider. It looked awful. Dead leaves lay all over everything, the vegetable garden was a mess, unspaded and littered with last year's stalks and vines that I hadn't got around to cleaning up before snowfall, and worst of all, the remains of an old log cabin that I'd had torn down the summer before were piled untidily alongside the woodshed. The logs were pine, sound and dry, and it had been my opinion that they were too good to waste, that they'd make wonderful kindling wood, when, as and if they were worked up into more suitable lengths than twenty feet.

For a moment my heart failed me. The yard I could rake, the garden I could spade, but the shambles by the woodshed I could never clean up in less than ten years. The people whom I had hired for the summer weren't coming In until the middle of June, which did me no good in my present straights, and I knew that I couldn't borrow a man from Larry, because he was in the midst of a busy spell. Then I thought of the log-drive and the river-hogs. Sometimes on a drive there are periods of several days when there is no work for the men, because the booms of logs that are coming down from the lakes up above have been held up by head winds. Until they arrive, the river-hogs—or log-drivers, if you prefer —just kill time, washing out their socks, playing poker, carving fancy bottle stoppers, and in general becoming more and more bored with themselves. We were in such a period then. So I called up the company clerk at the Middle Dam wangan and asked him if he had a couple of men who'd like to make a little money on the side cutting wood for me. He said he didn't know, but he'd inquire; and pretty soon two river-hogs came knocking at the door. They looked like ninety percent of the hundreds of their kind whom I have known in the time I have lived here, dressed in torn shirts, stagged pants, battered hats, gumboots, and four-day stubbles. They looked as though they'd just as soon murder you for a nickel as not; but I knew from experience that this appearance was deceptive, so I didn't yell bloody murder and slam the door in their faces. I went out into the yard and started to tell them what I wanted done.

That clerk apparently fancied himself as a humorist. Of the fifty men at his disposal, he sent me one who didn't have a word of English to his name, and one who was that rare thing, literally stone deaf. Of course neither of them could read, and the less said about my French the better. And there they stood looking at me, as eager to understand and to please as a pair of spaniels. I could cheerfully have garrotted that clerk. There was nothing for it but to resort to sign language, to get them started on the job, and then to take a quick trip to Middle Dam for a conference with Louie Boutin, who was working for Larry. He'd be willing to give me a brief boot-course in basic woods French. So I pointed to the wood, pointed to the saws and axes, pointed to the space where I wanted the split wood stacked, and made sawing, splitting, and stacking motions. I probably looked as silly as I felt, but their faces broke into sunny smiles, and they nodded vigorously and burst into a spate of French. It seemed to me that the intelligent question for men in their position to be asking should be into what lengths I wanted the wood sawed, so I held my hands about a foot apart, dived deep into my subconscious, and dragged up the phrase, "Comme ça." It worked. They seized a two-man crosscut and a saw horse, and did what is locally termed "flew at it." I flew into the Ford and up to Middle, besieged by misgivings.

I never had two more satisfactory people work for me. They ignored me almost completely and concentrated on the job. The Siases showed up a day early, so I started eating most of my meals and spending most of my time at the hotel, two miles away from my henchmen. It didn't make any difference to them. Judging from the results, I would say that they worked even harder when I wasn't around to keep an eye on them. I came home one afternoon to change my shirt and found that they'd finished the wood, raked up the yard without being told to, and were busy shoring up the top part of the woodshed, which I use for storage, and which needed bracing badly. When they heard me coming they rushed out into the driveway, obviously filled with glee and pride about something or other, although the only word I could catch out of the stream of French that was bubbling out of them was *porc-epic*. It developed that they'd done me the favor of killing four porcupines that were chewing the house down around my ears.

"Bonne!" I exclaimed, my courage, if not my French, fortified by my few sessions with Louie; and to be on the safe side grammatically, I added, "Très bien." This seemed inadequate, so I threw in for free, "Ah, mes braves hommes!" They burst into pleased laughter, which changed to guffaws when I let success go to my head and developed the theme: "Mes braves, aimants hommes." I should have let well enough alone. I meant *aimables*, I guess. They were gentlemen, though. They realized that anybody could make a slight error like that, saying "loving" when she meant "kind."

The next morning they showed up right after their breakfast to see what else I wanted done; or at least, I assumed that's what they wanted. I led them out to the garden and made a sweeping gesture. "Le jardin des legumes," I said grandly, and to be sure they understood, I showed them a boxful of gaudily illustrated packets of seeds I'd bought, cucumbers, lettuce, carrots, stringbeans, and what-all. They nodded, wreathed in smiles, and went off to the shop to get spading forks and rakes. After I'd eaten my own breakfast, I went off up to the hotel to play with my friends, leaving them hard at work. As it happened, I didn't get back until after dark, so I didn't see the garden again until morning. They had not only spaded it, but they'd banked it into raised beds, European style, and planted it for me. I never saw such a neat and attractive garden in my life, with the smallest pebbles raked off, and the empty packets fastened to whittled sticks at the end of each row, gaily indicating the nature of the future crop.

That was all the work I had for them to do, so I called up the clerk again and asked him to tell them to come down and get their pay. He laughed in what I thought was rather a snide manner. "What's the matter?" he asked. "Don't you like them?"

"Certainly I like them. They've been wonderful. They've worked themselves out of a job, that's all." I thought that ought to spoil his joke for him, but I added for good measure, "Gave me a chance to brush up on my French, too." That would fix his red wagon.

We had a little trouble over the pay. In the first place, I couldn't understand what they were trying to tell me, with the aid of the clock and held-up fingers except that it was the number of hours they had worked and the rate per hour. I kept saying "Combien?" which I thought meant "How much?"—and maybe it does; but that didn't get me anywhere. So finally I spread out all the cash I had, about twenty dollars, on the kitchen table, and indicated that they should take what was right. They picked up four and a half dollars apiece.

That was perfectly ridiculous for the amount of work they had done, so I started shaking my head and saying, "No, not enough." A little wistfully, they handed back the fifty cent pieces. I gave up, with a loud cry of "Mon Dieu!" took all the money away from them, and gave them each seven dollars. They were apparently pleased, and I certainly was. I'd never bought a bigger fourteen dollars' worth of labor. Until the drive ended and they took off for parts unknown, they " 'Ça-va?"-ed me enthusiastically every time they saw me along the road, and twice came down and weeded the garden, in which I suppose they took a proprietary interest, just for fun. They were nice men. They proved to me, at least, that a language barrier and the barrier of widely divergent backgrounds and interests need not prevent mutual understanding and esteem, if good will and a common goal exist.

They also demonstrated nicely two of the characteristics shared by everyone who has ever worked for me. One is absolute honesty in material matters. People lean over backwards to be honest. Once Whit Roberts ran out of cigarettes, so I loaned him a pack to see him through until the next day. About two months later, when I came to pay him off for the season, I added up my figures, showed them to him, and asked him if they were correct.

"Pretty near," he said. "Take off fifteen cents for them cigarettes I got off you back 'round the Fourth of July, and we'll call it square." I'd long ago forgotten all about them, and would have been glad to give them to him anyhow; but Whit wouldn't have it. He owed me for them and he was bound he'd pay. I've had women who worked for me trail me clear up to the spring on the ridge back of the house, through brambles and swamp, to ask me if it would be all right for them to borrow a length of my black thread with which to sew on a button. They knew perfectly well that it would be all right, but they weren't going meddling around other people's belongings without asking first. That's a very nice attitude to live with.

The other characteristic is absolute honesty in ethical matters. People around here don't seem to worry lest they do a little more work than they are paid for, or to try to gold-brick on the job, which is just the same as stealing money, since they are collecting pay for the time spent in loafing. Instead of considering things in the light of so much money for so much time put in, they see it as a unit of work to be done, and don't consider themselves through until it is done. I've more than once come upon one of the help doing something I had not told her to do. When I commented upon it, she'd be sure to say, "Well, you asked me to tidy up this cupboard, and when I got the dishes out, the paint looked kind of smudgy, so I thought I might as well make a job of it and wash it now, while it's handy." It's very comforting to know that you don't have to be a Simon Legree; that you don't have to hound and spy upon your help constantly; that they are not just going through motions, but are actually looking for things to do.

I remember only once having to give a direct order and insist upon its being carried out. It was one Sunday noon, when Whit and Gertie Roberts were working for me. Larry called up and wanted to know if Whit would be willing to take a boat down to South Arm that afternoon to make an emergency repair on the dock; and when I asked Whit, he said sure, tell Larry he'd leave right after dinner.

"You go, too, Gert," I said. "You haven't been off the

reservation for weeks, and it's a lovely day for a boat-ride. You can visit with Mrs. Graves while Whit fixes the float."

She looked at me, and at the sink piled with pots and pans, and at the uncleared table. "And who's going to do the dishes and get supper?" she asked, on a climbing inflection.

"I am," I told her.

"Well, I don't know—I hate to— Is that an *order?*"

"That's an order," I said. "Now get out from under my feet. Go on and have a good time."

She went, but I don't think she felt right about it.

Whit and Gertie have worked for me summers for a long time, and the longer I know them, the more I respect them. They are not young, being well into their sixties, with not too easy a life behind them. After all, they are the parents of seven adult children, and the grandparents of I don't know how many more; and by this time they may easily be great-grandparents as well. They've fed and clothed and educated their children, and seen them through long illnesses and expensive accidents, all on the not-exactly-stupendous wages of a country carpenter. What's more, every one of their children has turned out well, at least by my standards. It's true that none of them has become President of the United States, or amassed a million dollars, or won the Nobel Prize. But none of them has been in jail, or on public relief, or deported from the country, either. They are, each and every one of them, law-abiding, self-supporting, and self-respecting; in short, good, solid citizens. To me, beset by the problems and worries of bringing up only two children to be a credit to me—and more important, to themselves—and painfully conscious of how easily the best-intentioned parent can fail, it is a wonerful thing not to find one bad egg in a basket of seven.

Now that their children are all married or working away from home, Whit and Gertie are relaxing and pampering themselves a little. They are finally doing and having things that they have looked forward to all their lives. They own their own home in Andover, and it is a model of convenience and neatness, with a gorgeous big flower garden out to one side. They've put in a bathroom and electricity, and the reason that Gertie started working for me was that she'd made up her mind that she wanted an electric washing machine and re-frigerator. She considered them luxuries—she'd got along for fifty years with a big family, without them—so she didn't feel justified in asking Whit to buy them for her. Her view was that he worked hard enough already, without killing himself to keep her in expensive and unnecessary gadgets. She was able-bodied and would earn her own fripperies, thank you. And she did. Her husband was already working for me, and I was looking for a cook, so it seemed only sensible that she should enter my employ; sensible, and pleasant all around.

She gets through a terrific amount of work in a day, even up here, where housework isn't easy. We have no electricity, so when we do the washing, we use a gasoline washing ma-chine. That's all right, but sometimes you waste half the morning fooling with needle-valves and spark plugs, before you can start the motor and get on with your laundry. You have to heat all the water in copper boilers on a wood-burning range. Wash-day is a shambles around here, with the house-hold completely disorganized and a catch-as-catch-can dinner at noon, consisting of yesterday's cold roast, warmed-over potatoes and vegetables, and an assortment of desserts: one stray piece of pie, what was left of the brown-betty, one dish of chocolate pudding, and some cookies. As you can see, it's refrigerator-cleaning day, as well as wash-day. Then the ironing! We have to use what are fittingly named sad-irons, old-fashioned irons that must be heated on top of the range. They make for a long, hard ironing, I'm here to tell you.

I went into the kitchen one day and found Gertie painstakingly ironing what I thought was Rufus' underwear. "For the love of peace, Gert," I said, "what are you wasting time and energy on that kid's underwear for, the way he treats it? He doesn't have to have it ironed."

She went on ironing, looking a little embarrassed as she put a knife crease into a pair of shorts. "It isn't Rufus'," she admitted. "It's Whitney's. I suppose it's foolish, but even when the children were little and goodness knows I had my hands full, I've always ironed his underwear. Not that he'd complain if I didn't; but I know he likes it ironed, and it seems little enough to do for him." That's the sort of trivial but important thing that makes so many marriages in this country last for fifty years, growing better all the time.

I think Whit and Gert are wonderful together anyhow, although they probably won't thank me for saying so. I envy them lots of times, as for example one Sunday late in September, when my children had gone Out to school and the three of us were here alone. It was a simply heavenly day, bright and blue, with the sun gilding the first-turning autumn leaves, and the air sparkling and crisp. After breakfast I decided I would go up to Middle Dam to see the Siases, who had come back for the fall fishing. Gertie was just getting the roast for dinner out of the refrigerator when I announced this plan.

"Are you going to eat up there?" she asked.

"I don't know yet," I told her. "I haven't got that far. Why?"

"Well, nothing, really. Only if you weren't going to be home, I wouldn't cook this meat until to-morrow."

"But you and Whit have to eat."

"Well, yes. But if you were going to eat at the hotel, we thought we'd put up a lunch and go off somewhere on a picnic. I do love a picnic."

"For Heaven's sake!" I said. "Why didn't you say so before? You go ahead. I will eat at Middle."

I got home before they did, late in the afternoon, and pretty soon I heard them coming up the Carry, laughing together like a couple of kids. They came in with their hair windblown and their noses sunburned, carrying Whit's hat full of late blueberries, a big bunch of goldenrod and wild asters, and a little homemade birch-bark basket full of ferns, which they gave me for the fireplace mantel. And I thought then that if I could look forward with any certainty to having such a good time as they had, twenty-five years hence, I'd be willing to go through all the work and grief and worry they must have gone through together.

Whit is the best workman I have ever seen, bar none. There is something completely fascinating to me in watching anyone who knows his trade, whatever it may be. I think I admire competence in any line more than I do any other attribute. I like people who know what they're doing, and who go about doing it with no fuss or feathers. There is something proud and integrated about them, some quality of modesty and assurance that sets them apart from ordinary dubs in an aristocracy of their own, no matter how humble that trade may be considered generally. Whit is supposed to be a carpenter, but he would be called a cabinet-maker anywhere else. Apparently he can't do a slap-dash piece of work. I once asked him if he'd please nail up a few old boards into a hutch for some rabbits the children owned, and when I examined the finished product, I almost wouldn't let the rabbits set foot in it. It was too beautiful to waste on rabbits, with the corners mitred perfectly and finished with quarter-rounds, and the rough edges of the boards planed down to a satin smoothness. But since I couldn't get into it myself, I finally let them have it.

My kitchen floor had long been a source of pain to me. It had been put down originally as a temporary expedient, and was made of rough planks. Not only did it look terrible, but it was impossible to keep clean, and furthermore had a tendency to warp and curl, presenting hazards to trip the unwary. I finally decided I couldn't put up with it a minute longer, and after a conference with Whit, I went up to Middle Dam to use their Outside line to call the lumberyard. Whit and I had decided that soft wood was good enough for a kitchen, but when I went into a huddle with Lester Farrington, the dealer, over the telephone, I discovered that the price of even second-grade soft wood was appalling. It was the war, Lester said.

"I might just as well pave my floor with gold bricks and be done with it," I said. "That's altogether too much money." He said he agreed with me completely, and, if he were I, he'd wait until after the war, when prices would probably go down. I went home and gave Whit the bad news. He said, "Oh," and sat on a chopping block, whistling under his breath and jiggling his foot up and down. Experience had taught me that these were the outward manifestations of deep thought, so I went away.

Finally he came looking for me, and announced, "You know, Louise, you've got that left-over hardwood flooring up in the shop attic." I didn't know any such thing. I leave matters like that to those who understand them. "I've just measured it up, and there's almost enough for the kitchen. I know hardwood's dear, but 'twouldn't cost you much to buy what little more you need. Only thing is, that flooring was bought a long time ago, when things were better. It's really too good to put down in a kitchen. Seems a shame to abuse it."

I said we might as well use it in the kitchen where we needed it, rather than let it lie idle in the shop forever, so that's what we did. Whit laid it, scraped it down, and put on a coat of pre-war tung oil finish that I got from Larry. We ate sandwiches on the porch that day, instead of a nice hot dinner, to avoid conflict with his project. When it was done, it looked wonderful—the color of dark honey, with the straight, fine grain brought up nicely—and I said so.

"Really ought to have another coat," he said. "One coat won't stand up good, especially in a kitchen, with people tracking in and spilling water all over. It'd pay you to let me put on a second coat." This sounded sensible to me, so a couple of days later we had another cold dinner, and Whit put on another coat. The floor looked even more wonderful than before. We hated to walk on it. But Whit took to eyeing it moodily. At last, out of a clear sky, he said, "What this floor really ought to have is a rubbing down with fine sandpaper, and a top coat of finish. Then you'd really have a floor."

"It looks better than any other floor in the house already," I said. "Is it really necessary?"

"Well, no. Not what you might call necessary. But that there's beautiful wood, not like the trash they sell you nowadays, and it seems kind of a pity—"

"If it's not necessary, I guess we won't bother," I announced heartlessly. "I've got too many other things in mind that I want to get done this season." And that seemed to be that.

That evening when Gertie and I sat on the porch after supper, reading the paper and relaxing, Whit failed to join us. I assumed he'd gone fishing, and even when it became dark enough for us to move into the house and light the lamps, I didn't question his not putting in an appearance. He quite often goes to bed before it's dark under the table, as we say here. But at ten o'clock, when I went down into the kitchen to get a drink of water, I heard a strange, steady, shushing sound going on down there. It was Whit, busily sanding down the floor by lamplight. He just couldn't bear to allow a good job to fall short of being beautiful, just for lack of a little more time and care spent on it. He rubbed the floor down and put on the extra coat of finish on his own time, and felt that his personal satisfaction in a job done right was ample pay.

Whit can do anything, even if he is supposed to be only a carpenter. He can paint and tinker gasoline motors into running and handle any kind of a boat and hunt and fish and trap and knit socks and garden, among other things. The only thing he can't do is drive a car. I was trying, one day, to talk him into learning to drive the Ford. I pointed out that it would be much more convenient and perhaps even safer if there were two of us in the household who could drive. He said no. He didn't want to learn. He'd rather walk where he had to go than drive a car. He didn't have any sympathy with automobiles, so he doubted if he'd be able to learn anyhow.

"That's nonsense, Whitney," I said. "You're crazy about motorboats. You run them all the time. If you want to go across the lake, you don't feel that you have to row—or swim. What's the difference? And as for not being able to learn to drive: anybody who can run that damn kicker-boat of yours can run anything."

"I ever tell you about my grandfather?" he asked, in what seemed to be a non sequitur, but I was sure was not. Whit either talks to the point or keeps still.

"The one that took one drink a year, before Christmas dinner?"

"Nope, that was my father. Wouldn't eat his dinner, either, 'less his drink was forthcoming. No, my grandfather that put me in the habit of eating my pie backwards."

"Oh, sure." I knew about that grandfather. When Whit was a child, almost seventy years ago, his grandfather had always made him eat a piece of pie from the thick end of the wedge toward the point, so that there'd be no last-minute decisions that he was too full to finish the crust. Whit does it automatically to this day, and so do my own children, who learned the trick from him. "What about him?"

"Well, he used to work for the Whitneys, owned that big summer place up by Mosquito Brook in the Narrows. Worked there for years. That's how I got my name, Whitney, after them. Anyway, one thing my grandfather wouldn't do was wheel a wheelbarrow. Don't know the whys and wherefores of it, but somewhere or other he'd got a terrible nif against the things, and he wouldn't have no truck with them. Old Man Whitney naturally found out about it in the course of the years, and he'd try to finagle things so my grandfather'd have to give in and use a wheelbarrow, but my grandfather always managed somehow to weasel out of it. Finally the Old Man bought one, a big enormous heavy one, and had the boatman put it together on the boat, coming up from the Arm. When the boat come in, Old Man Whitney told my grandfather to go down to the dock and bring up the freight, like he always done. You ever been up to Whitney's? Then you know what a long, up-hill haul it is from the landing to the house. Well, my grandfather went down, all unsuspecting, and the Old Man and the family and the guests lined up on the porch to see the fun and give my grandfather a horse-laugh. Bimeby they see my grandfather coming up from the dock. He had the wheelbarrow, all right. But he was carrying it on his back. Awkward thing to carry, too, and it must have weighed over a hundred pounds. Old Man Whitney give up, after that."

I laughed. I could just see that stubborn old Yankee struggling up the steep and stony trail, bowed under the load, but unbroken in spirit.

Whit looked dreamily out across the river. "There's an awful lot of my grandfather in me," he remarked softly.

I never again brought up the subject of his learning to drive the Ford.

Of all the people who have worked for me, I guess I entertain as kindly a feeling for Merle Hodge as for any, in spite of the fact that he worked here only one summer. He had been guiding at the hotel, but when the warmer weather spoiled the fishing, the guiding business went into a slump. One night when I was collecting my mail at Middle, I asked Al if she knew of anyone I could hire to help Whit with a fieldstone fireplace and chimney he was building for me. That's a two-man job. She said Merle was leaving, and maybe he'd like the job; and it turned out that he would. So he came down and stayed until October. He was in his late twenties, a veteran, and possessed the same kind of sense of humor I fancy I have. I had a lot of fun with Merle, especially after I discovered that it annoyed him when I prefaced any bit of advice I was going to hand out by saying, "Now, Merle, I'm almost old enough to be your mother, and I want you to pay attention to what I say."

But that isn't why I esteemed Merle so. It started with the Reo. I have an old Model A pick-up which everybody uses for errands and running up and down the road, and what used to be a Reo Speed-wagon, about twenty years ago. Ralph however rebuilt it, stripping it down, removing the back springs so that the rear end would stay down if you happened to be dragging logs behind it, and putting in a second transmission. This gives it forty-seven speeds forward and twenty-nine backwards, more or less, by various combinations of gears, and makes it possible to haul tons of dead weight at any speed from two miles an hour to a hundred. It is an awkward, homely-looking thing, and uncomfortable for anyone except the driver to ride in, but I love the Reo. It simply shouts of power, and I like to feel all those horses at my command. When I start out for anywhere in the Reo, I'm always sure I'm going to get there.

When Merle first came down to Forest Lodge, I took him around and showed him the equipment he'd be using. "The Ford you know about," I said, "but I'll have to explain the Reo to you." I showed him how it worked, and concluded my little homily, "She's *my* baby. I'm very much attached to this old jallopy."

Merle looked at it coldly. "I'll take the Ford," he said.

One Sunday afternoon about a month later, I decided to take the kids swimming down-river. I told everyone where I was going, and Merle asked, "Do you mind if I take one of the cars and go up to Middle to shoot the breeze with the boys?" I said of course not, and which car did he want?

"Makes no difference to me," he said. "Which one are you going to use?"

I said it made no difference to me either. I'd take the one he didn't want. We batted that back and forth for a while, until I could see that we were both being too polite to get us anywhere, so I said I'd take the Ford. It was more comfortable for the kids, riding in back.

"Good," said Merle, looking happy.

"What do you mean, *good?*" I demanded. "I thought you didn't like the Reo."

He had the grace to look slightly abashed. "Well, I'll tell you, Louise. That Reo sort of grows on you." It did me a lot of good to find someone, at last, after all the sneers and scorn that have been heaped on the Reo, that felt the same way about it that I do.

Then Larry called up one day and wanted to know what Merle was doing. I told him, and he asked if I could possibly spare him for a few days. A party wanted a guide, and he was fresh out of guides. If I'd loan him Merle— We're always loaning our help back and forth, and it always makes me feel slightly guilty, as though I were Trafficking in Human Flesh. However, I said sure, if Merle wanted to be loaned. He did, changed from his old blue concrete-mixing shirt into his bright plaid guiding shirt, and went off up to Middle Dam. In the evening after work he came home to make a call on us. He sat down in the living room with a purposeful air, and said, "Louise, teach me about fishing."

That did it. That made Merle my friend for life. Actually

he knows much more about fishing than I do, and all he wanted
to learn was where in these waters, which are unfamiliar to him,
the best places are in the fall. But I don't care what the ex-
tenuating circumstances may be. Someone has asked *me* to
teach him about fishing.

These men—these and others like them—are the people with
whom I live in closest intimacy, an intimacy unavoidable in
this country no matter how large your house may be, between
employer and employed. We have to live in each others'
pockets, as we say. During working hours we may retire
each to his own private world of interest; but when the work
is done and the sun drops down behind Inlet Ridge and the
forest starts inching closer and closer to the house, then we
are driven inside the stockade, inside the four walls and the
roof that keep at bay the wilderness and the weather. It is
then, under the merciless test of familiarity, that our weaknesses are exposed to each other and our strengths revealed.
Whether the house stands or falls depends upon the nature of
those strengths and weaknesses. My house still stands. I have
been fortunate in my hired help.

12

Well You May Ask

IT IS UNFORTUNATELY true that the writer seldom does what
he wants to do; he only does the best he can. Within his heart
and mind are feelings and ideas which he wishes to convey;
which, indeed, he *must* at least attempt to convey, since he
acts under a real compulsion which he cannot deny and remain whole. These ideas may not be important to anyone else,
but they are important enough to the writer so that he is willing to spend a great deal of time and energy—and yes, mental
anguish, exaggerated as that may sound—on their proper expression, in order that they may be shared with others. Usually
he is only partly successful, and that is what makes writing,
much of the time, a painful and frustrating occupation: the
fact that the product of the labor, in cold print, falls so far
short of the living, glowing concept. When I read over what
I have written, I ordinarily feel just as I do when I try to sing,
only worse, because I don't pretend to be a singer and I do
try to think that I'm a writer. I can run through whole arias
in my head, hearing the full, rich, pear-shaped tones as clearly
as anything; and then when I open my mouth all that comes
out is a thin, reedy, pitiful squawk. It's damn discouraging.
The compensation of writing, I ought to add, comes once in a

blue moon, when you recognize with a certainty that nothing can shake that you have somehow managed, for once, to say exactly what you wanted to say, have portrayed a character exactly as he is, have painted a scene in its true colors. Those are the moments which deter a writer from pitching his typewriter into the river and starting to take in washing, as being an easier and surer way of earning a living.

When I set out to write this book, I knew exactly what I wanted to do. It had occurred to me that while I had written before of my life and the country here, I had been too selfishly preoccupied with my own problems and the background against which they have been—more or less—successfully solved to have paid proper attention to one of the chief factors in making that life good, or even possible for me: my friends and neighbors. I wanted—and it sounds quite simple—to tell about them in such a way that others could know and appreciate what kind of people they are and why I admire them so much. I wish, in justice to my friends, that I could have done better; but perhaps God is the only one with the necessary knowledge and equipment to do justice to even ordinary people.

And these people are ordinary people, like the large majority of their compatriots, quietly going about their business from day to day, doing their best to get along. Not one of them is individually significant on the national scene, or even on the miniature scene of local affairs. Not one of them wants to be, or tries to be, "important." But it seems to me that they are nevertheless important, because they are, in a time and country where so many are selling themselves down the river for a materialistic and shoddy way of life, the last exponents of the qualities and standards and virtues upon which this nation was founded. I do not say that here alone still exists the attitude that puts character above personality, principle above expediency, duty above pleasure, and independence above ease. It may easily be true of other places. I think that it must be true of other places where people live as we do here, close to the soil and seasons, close to each other, if not geographically, certainly spiritually, far enough removed from the stress and speed of modern living so that we have time to form our own considered opinions and freedom to act in accordance with them.

I read something in Ruskin once that seems to me to apply to the kind of people this country breeds, the simple, deliberate, durable people: "No changing of place at a hundred miles an hour will make us one whit stronger, happier or wiser. The really precious things are thought and sight, not pace. It does a bullet no good to go fast; and a man, if he be truly a man, no harm to go slow; for his glory is not at all in going, but in being."

It may be that these qualities which I so admire and which were commonly possessed in the early days of this country's history survive here as an anachronism. It may be that they are no longer necessary in the world of to-day, where man's worst enemies are himself and his misuse of his own expanding knowledge, enemies which possibly must be fought with different and more subtle weapons than the simple ones necessary to keep at bay the simpler foes, the wilderness and the weather. But it seems to me equally possible that these qualities possessed by my people, the kind of people whom I like and understand, may be the pinch of yeast in the bit of dough, with which, when the time is ripe, the whole mass will become leaven. When humanity gets tired enough of being hounded from pillar to post, when the powerful have sufficiently persecuted the weak and the envious weak have sufficiently obstructed the strong, perhaps our way of life will come to seem the true one, the good one; and people everywhere will awake in astonishment at having for so long neglected its simple wisdom.

THE END